The College Unicorn

Exposing the Myth of College and Career Planning

William Roberts Jr. & Anthony Meister

ISBN-10: 1468133519
ISBN-13: 978-1468133516

Contents

FOREWORD

We have set forth some radical ideas in this book. The content reflects the current beliefs and opinions of the authors. The authors are not career counselors, guidance counselors, or psychologists.

The motivation behind *The College Unicorn* is fueled by concerned parents who believe the world has changed such that a new approach to college education is required.

We aspire to have this book serve as a guideline to positive changes in a student's attitude, college and career planning roadmap, and his or her personal financial management.

Those who we have quoted in this book may not share our exact beliefs and opinions. May this book become a call to action, dialogue, and debate.

Chapter 1
Money Isn't Everything

"All animals are equal but some animals are more equal than others." -George Orwell, Animal Farm

Money may not be "everything," but money, or earning power, should be considered the highest priority in college or career planning. After all, isn't it assumed that if someone has a "good job" they're probably making a decent salary?

You really don't *need* money to enjoy life. It's true for some, but having money does solve many problems, and once solved, personal freedom and enjoyment follow.

When picking a college subject major, it's typically more about what the student "wants to be when they grow up," and less consideration is given to his or her future personal financial freedom and lifestyle.

The required emphasis on earning power is lacking, because a lot of us are simply bad with money. Many people diligently fail to make wise daily financial decisions. Many of us don't save properly, we take on too much debt, and we usually blow any extra money instead of investing it.

To be fair, not everyone is brought up in a household that openly discusses family finances, career planning, lifestyle design, and budgeting decisions. In fact, the majority of the time, it's the opposite.

Over and above poor money management, there are other reasons only about 10 percent of Americans become financially independent. People tend to harbor negative emotional thoughts about money; they don't like talking about it, fearing mutual embarrassment if they were to disclose their personal finances. The very topic of money in many social circles is taboo. Even discussions about money with a spouse can lead to arguments or tension.

Most say that they *want* more money, but at the same time, some of those people also harbor negative connotations about wealth.

It's common practice for us to believe that money doesn't buy happiness. You can't take money with you when you're dead, and it's the root of all evil.

Ask yourself: "Do I think this way about money, simply because I'm just like the other 90 percent of people around me?" ... "Does that mean that I'm actually **broke**?"

To fully appreciate the word "broke," you'll need to consider that there are different levels of being "broke" based on an individual's perception.

There's "I can't pay the electric bill""-going-to-die-freezing broke; or you may be lacking at least three months of income in the bank; or perhaps your "being broke" is knowing you haven't saved enough to retire when you want to. The point is that being "broke" could mean something specifically different, but it generally means that you're not financially independent. Whatever your level of "broke" might be, it's usually the result of poorly made financial decisions.

These everyday worries represent different realities, but in our view, about 90 percent of us are broke. We're broke and enslaved because we can't escape our seemingly hopeless situation of exchanging the best years of our life for money.

If we're not making enough money in exchange for that time, then we're actually not doing well at all. We're most likely going to miss out on the better lifestyle options that this world has to offer. We won't know about the possibility of a new reality because our awareness isn't centered correctly.

If we want to live worry-free, we need to shake the notion that money isn't really that important in life.

As someone living the "middle class" lifestyle, we think we're "doing okay." Things could get worse; we're not exactly sleeping on the streets. We probably have a working vehicle, a place to live, some savings, and a means to get a decent income. There's food on the table every night. As a matter of fact, you may even have enough money to put your children through college. You're probably reading this book because you hope that your kids will have a better life than you. Judging by your parents standards and the people around you, you probably think that you're doing just fine. You may even consider yourself "well off" at this point in time.

We think that we're doing alright because we're comparing ourselves to our own reference group. We're in denial because everyone we know is actually broke, just like us.

Most of us are comfortable being mediocre. Personally, I've been comfortable being average in the past. Looking back, it might have been that I was just lazy. The fundamental changes that I needed to bring into my life revolved around my attitude. My mindset changed when I really started to consider how I spent most of my time, my actual net worth, my dependence upon a salary, relationships, vacation schedules, insurance, fitness, benefits, freedom, hobbies, and toys.

I found that my current positions were not meeting up with my future expectations. Only then was it important enough to me that I would consider changing. It's hard to step back and look sometimes, but it must be done.

If you want a better lifestyle for your children, or yourself, you'll need to first define what exactly it is that will make it better.

Usually, it's more money, but instead of guessing at a number, you'll want to look at where your kids think they might live, what kind of car they'll drive, how many kids they'll have, and what type of vacations they'll go on. You'll need to help your student paint a picture of their future life exceeding the lifestyle they were brought up in. After you've talked about these factors, figure out what type of salary they'll need to support this lifestyle. A great tool to put a general number to your student's lifestyle salary requirements can be found at www.lifestylecalculator.com

Everyone's definition of being "rich" or "well off" is going to be different, just the same as everyone's definition of being broke. It's a valuable exercise to step back and view the world through the lens of the super-wealthy. It's not about being jealous—it's about realizing there is better available.

You will not know how bad you have it until you see how well others do. For example, if you spent your entire life being raised as an African bushman, you might still think that airplanes are gods, know how to make poison arrows, and imagine bacteria as evil spirits. There would be a tremendous impact to a Bushman's lifestyle if you shared with them the simple luxury of a cigarette lighter.

There's a huge difference between the rural lifestyle of a African tribesman and the modern lifestyle of a rich American. There are equal lifestyle disparities between living in third-world countries and living almost anywhere in the United States. There are many factors that impact lifestyle quality and local economies, so there will always be fluctuations.

In the United States we cover a wide scope of lifestyles, from having people who live on the streets to others who excel to greatness. The primary influence on lifestyle quality in our country continues to be earning power and solid financial management.

The wealthy are all around you, but your house probably isn't next to one of theirs; it's mathematically logical that you don't work together directly; and it's likely that you're not in their social circle. It's not typical to see a wealthy individual wandering the streets with cardboard signs, delivering your pizza, serving in the military, or even managing a Sprint PCS store.

If you're not financially well off, then it's fair to say your social circle is not financially independent. If you don't have wealthy people in your immediate reference group, it only makes sense that you won't be able to learn from them.

Most of the people with little money—most of us—are all around you. They're just like you, because they're just like their parents and friends. Birds of a feather—you are your own reference group.

Success guru Brian Tracy, a consultant to thousands of companies and top-selling author of more than forty-five books on business, economics, psychology, history, and philosophy, put it best by saying, "You're likely to earn an average of the salaries of your five closest friends." Is that true for you? It's probably true because of the way wealth is currently divided in America.

The fact is that over the last three decades, wealth in the US (defined as net worth) is concentrated in the top 10 percent of the population. In 1983, 68.2 percent of the net worth of the US was held by the top 10 percent of the population. By 2007, 73.1 percent of the net worth of the US was held by the top 10 percent of the population. When you hear or read the phrase "the rich are getting richer," it's a true statement and the trend has been quite consistent throughout the years.

The Levy Economics Institute published a working paper- *Recent Trends in Household Wealth in the United States: Rising Debt and the Middle-Class-Squeeze—an Update to 2007* by Edward N. Wolff

(No.589). The following is an excerpt from this report. Please focus on the last underlined sentence—

Previous work of mine…presented evidence of sharply increasing household wealth inequality between 1983 and 1989, followed by a modest rise between 1989 and 1998. Both mean and median wealth holdings climbed briskly during the 1983–1989 period. From 1989 to 1998, mean wealth continued to surge while median net worth rose at a rather anemic pace. <u>Indeed, the only segment of the population that experienced large gains in wealth from 1983 to 1998 was the richest 20 percent of households.</u>

Figure 1. Levy Economics Graph (Table 9 from the original report)

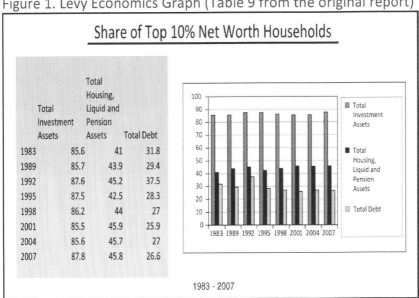

To simplify the report's findings, financial independence accrues to the top 10 percent of our society. Looking at the graph in Figure 1, you can see that landing yourself, or your child, in that top 10 percent of earners is the ticket to sustained wealth and a better life.

During the writing of this book, a political debate is taking place on this topic called "The Occupy Movement," protesting the difference between the 1 percent and 99 percent of United States income earners. We're not saying it's good or bad to have the wealth distributed the way it's currently trending. We're taking the stance that worry-free financial independence is concentrated in the top 10 percent of the population, and recognizing this trend, you should seek to achieve at that level.

Income trends support that a smaller percentage of the population will hold the majority of the wealth. A recent article from *CNN Money,* "How the Rich Became the Uber Rich," explains:

There's a growing income gap in America, but it's not necessarily between the rich and the poor. It's between the super rich and everyone else. Or as President George W. Bush once quipped at a swanky campaign dinner, "the haves and the have-mores."

The truth is that wealth in America consistently concentrates itself toward the top 10 percent of the population, and has trended that way for the last 40 years! The remaining 90 percent has always been financially stagnant or broke. To clarify, we're using the 90/10 split as an approximation. It's not exactly 90/10, but it's close and it makes the numbers easier to mentally digest.

"Insanity: Doing the same thing over and over again and expecting different results." – Albert Einstein

If you're following the same game plan that your parents told you to follow, you'll probably get similar results.

If you're currently in the bottom 90 percent, you're an economic slave. As a "90 percenter" you may think that it's unfair to be wealthy, money is the root of all evil, and the rich are greedy bullies. Even if that's the case, you must realize that the way money is separated in America leads to the following conclusion:

If You're Not Making Enough Money, You're Vulnerable to Becoming an Economic Slave.

Think about what that means…

- **Wealth in America is trending toward the top earners, meaning the top 10 percent of the population will increasingly possess more of our nation's wealth.**
- **Wealth at the 10 percent level, or above, provides lifestyle, career, and financial independence.**
- **If you earn in the bottom 90 percent, your net worth is less likely to increase, so you're unlikely to enjoy career and financial independence.**
- **Career and financial independence allows us to execute our life plans worry-free.**
- **Career and financial independence insulates us from economic uncertainty**.

You don't need to be an economist to fully appreciate this breakthrough understanding and apply it to career planning. However, it's paramount that you grasp the math involved. The reason we need to fully understand this is so you focus on the top 10 percent as the goal for your children and not accept settling for less.

If you're willing to have your child settle for less than earning a top 10 percent income, **stop reading this book**. **Don't even bother with college and don't waste your time with career planning.** You won't need any effort to be like everyone else, because it's easy.

If your student wants to strive to be a 10 percent earner, just showing up to college and collecting a degree isn't enough. It's likely to leave you with missed opportunities, debt, and set on the path to going broke while trying to be middle class.

Ninety percent of people think about college as the end goal. It's a tragic fallacy to believe that a college education, in itself, leads to career success. College degrees are no longer a magical unicorn that will get your graduate the job they need to reach the top 10 percent.

We know this is true, because students are moving back home with their parents after graduation. The debt students incur from their educations are rising while the employment opportunities that offer upward mobility for the middle class are decreasing. Student debt in America recently topped One Trillion Dollars, exceeding credit card debt. Some senior citizens are having their social security checks garnished to pay off student loans. From 2008 – 2010 tuition increased by about 15%. This trend is becoming a crisis. We'll get into the problems and solutions of college and the economy throughout the remaining chapters. Right now, I want you to conceptualize college as an investment. As with any investment, you would expect a return for risking your money upfront.

College = Investment

Michael Ellsberg, bestselling author and expert on career success, recently released his second book which is related to career planning: *"The Education of Millionaires: It's Not What You Think, and It's Not Too Late"*. Mr. Ellsberg's provocative and wise book primarily covers the idea of creating career success without a traditional college education. He provides a blueprint consisting of interviews and proven examples. The following is a paraphrased viewpoint that compares the college investment to making an investment in a start-up company:

I have the perfect investment opportunity for you. It's a start-up company and you can get in early before everyone else.

The company doesn't have a product, marketing skills, or sales ability. It doesn't know anything about basic finance, and the CEO doesn't really know what she wants to do tomorrow. She doesn't have a game plan to take the start-up company to the next level beyond your initial investment. That being said, you can have a good share of equity for as little as $40,000 to $175,000 if you write a check today.

Don't worry, we know you don't have the cash in hand, so we'll lend it to you. We know that borrowing to invest generally isn't a good idea, but don't worry, the interest is super-low. You don't need to think about the responsibility of paying your new debt if the company fails for a few years, because we'll delay the interest. The only warning is that if this start-up does fail, you'll be completely liable for the debt, and you wouldn't even be able to shake the responsibility with bankruptcy.

Ready to sign?

This is an example of the poor investment parents proudly make every year in their child's ill-researched career choice.

If your plan is the "College and Pray" approach, you may want to rethink your strategy.

The focus of this book is to help you realize that strategically and systematically working toward a place in the top 10 percent of post-college earners is worth it. After you've made that realization, you can leverage the tools and resources we've put together for you.

We've collected a vast wealth of data, interviewed successful people, talked with college and career experts, and condensed it into this guide, which if followed, will assist in your student's career success.

This goal isn't merely an income number, but a state of mind. It's an understanding that being financially secure is important. It's important because it means liberation from pulling the plow of regret. Having freedom to enjoy both the simple pleasures *and* the luxuries of life. This is why it's important to know the cost, resolve to pay it, and make a plan.

We shouldn't need to sell you on the idea that it's a good thing to make more money than other people. You already know that there's an obvious benefit. But have you experienced what it's like to truly not to worry about money? When you're a top 10 percent earner who manages your money well, you're then able to enjoy more and worry less. The $50K to $250K question is: What can one do so my student graduates from college in the top 10 percent of income earners?

Chapter 2
The Top Ten Percent

I always knew I was going to be rich. I don't think I ever doubted it for a minute. −Warren Buffett

<u>Who are they? How'd they get there? We can learn from them!</u>

We can assume that if you're reading this you've decided that a career plan designed to land your child in to the top 10 percent is a worthwhile pursuit. If the goal is the top 10 percent, then it's a good idea to get acquainted with who's already there.

We've established that the concentration of wealth increases to this particular group. These are the individuals who live life "worry free," or at least free from concern about a fluctuating economy or dependence on others for employment.

As you may have deduced already, it is the connected, influential individuals, and even entire families, who typically occupy this upper level of financial success and wealth creation. They have been managing their success, wealth, and power, not only for themselves, but for future generations. They have been passing down these life lessons to their children as well. We have done extensive research into a great number of these families. This research includes, but is not limited to, their common traits, strategies, and accomplishments.

What follows are numerous examples of these individuals and families who have demonstrated a consistent ability to not only achieve financial and career independence, but maintain this level of success year after year, and for generations. I've chosen many who are "household" names, but I have also chosen some who may not be familiar. These lesser-known examples equally exemplify the characteristics of all those in the top 10 percent.

Some that I included you may not "like"—that is, you may not agree with their politics or beliefs. But let me remind you that Optimal Career Planning is a program that transcends politics, religion, and social opinion. As a result we provide these examples in order to extract common practices and strategies that have become the underpinnings for "The Pathways to the Top 10 Percent." By reading these examples you too will have the confidence to trust the specific "pathway" you select knowing it is time-tested, and knowing it's served as the "pathway" for those who are already there.

Before reading these specific case studies, I'll dispel one possible early conclusion. An assumption that these examples involve what is sometimes termed as "old money," and all we're doing is pointing out the success of those who already were born with a "silver spoon." For them, entry into the top 10 percent was predestined, and that without such a legacy, anyone else's entry in to the top 10 percent is unlikely.

Let me reassure you, Optimal Career Planning is here to promote the exact opposite of such a notion. Not only is reaching the top 10 percent possible, it is guaranteed when you combine native ability, hard work, a directed career plan, and lifelong learning in the art of success.

To prove that this segment of the population is just waiting for you, please consider the information from a recent article on the business website CNN Money. In "The Coming Millionaire Boom" (Dickler, May 9, 2011), the total number of families in the U.S. with a net worth of over $1 million will double by 2020, as stated by the Deloitte Center for Financial Services, reaching 20.6 million. This is up from 12.7 million millionaire households in 2006.

So, according to the experts, it is possible for you and your child to plan and achieve financial independence! And this isn't something that one has to wait for the time to be "right,"—this increase in the concentration of wealth and the number of wealthy is on an accelerated track!

With no time to waste, let's move on to the case studies of those who've already made it there. I'll make some introductions, and then we'll look at their history and accomplishments. We've cherry-picked some excellent examples and then tied the common threads together so that your future collegian can chart a course to the top 10 percent.

The Rothschilds

Dating back to the Ottoman Empire, the Rothschild family settled in Venice. There, they started banking operations, later spreading across Europe, making Venice the banking capital of Europe. The Rothschild family dominated the banking scene across Europe, and has been the sole creditors to the empires of Britain and Bavaria. The name of Rothschild carries a heavyweight title throughout the banking sector in today's world.

Edmond de Rothschild (1926–1997)

Educated at Geneva University and obtaining a law degree in Paris, he founded the LCF Rothschild Group in 1953, based in Geneva, with $100 billion in assets. Today it extends to fifteen countries across the world. The LCF Rothschild Group's committee is currently being chaired by Benjamin de Rothschild, Edmond's son.

Jacob Rothschild (Born 1936)

In 1980, he resigned from N M Rothschild & Sons and took independent control of RIT Capital Partners, one of the UK's largest investment trusts. He went on to found St. James's Place Capital in

1991. In December 2009, Jacob Rothschild invested $200 million of his own money in North Sea Oil Company.

Édouard de Rothschild (Born 1957)

Édouard de Rothschild is a businessman belonging to the French branch of the prominent Rothschild family. Édouard studied law in France and in 1985 graduated with an MBA degree from the Stern School of Business at New York University.

David de Rothschild (Born 1978)

David de Rothschild, the youngest heir to his family's banking fortune, was born in London, England. As a teenager, de Rothschild was a top-ranked horse jumper on Britain's junior event team. He later gave up the sport to pursue his education, stating in an interview with *The New Yorker*, "I realized there was more to life than spending hours and hours and hours on a horse." After leaving Harrow School in 1996 he attended Oxford Brookes, receiving a BS (Honors) in political science and information systems. In 2002, he studied at the College of Naturopathic Medicine, London, where he received an advanced Diploma in natural medicine.

In January 2010, **Nathaniel Philip Rothschild** bought a substantial share of the Glencore mining and oil company. In late 2010, **Baron Benjamin Rothschild** said that the family had been unaffected by the financial crisis of 2007–2010.

The Rockefellers

The combined wealth of the family—its total assets and investments plus the individual wealth of its members—has never been known with any precision. Independent researchers have valued the current assets of the Rockefeller family as high as $110 billion. Management of this fortune today also rests with professional money managers who oversee the principal holding company, Rockefeller Financial Services, which controls all the family's investments. The present chairman is <u>David Rockefeller Jr.</u>

A trademark of the dynasty over its 140-plus years has been the remarkable family unity it has maintained. A primary reason has been the lifelong efforts of John D. Rockefeller Jr. to forge family unity even as he allowed his five sons to operate independently. This was also because of the high value placed on family unity, first by Nelson and John the Third, and later with David Rockefeller.

John D. Rockefeller (1839–1937)

John Rockefeller attended Cleveland's Central High School and then took a ten-week business course at <u>Folsom's Commercial College</u> where he studied bookkeeping. In September 1855, when Rockefeller was sixteen, he got his first job as an assistant <u>bookkeeper</u>. He was particularly adept at calculating transportation costs, which served him well later in his career. In February 1865, Rockefeller established the firm of Rockefeller & Andrews, an oil refinery. Rockefeller said, "It was the day that determined my career." He was well-positioned to take advantage of postwar prosperity and the great expansion westward, fostered by the growth of <u>railroads</u> and an <u>oil</u>-fueled economy. He borrowed heavily, reinvested profits, adapted rapidly to changing markets, and fielded observers to track the quickly expanding industry.

John D. Rockefeller Jr. (1874–1960)

Initially Rockefeller Jr. had intended to go to <u>Yale</u> but was encouraged by <u>William Rainey Harper</u>, president of the <u>University of Chicago</u>, among others, to enter the Baptist-oriented <u>Brown University</u> instead. He joined both the glee and the mandolin clubs, taught a Bible class, and was elected junior class president. Scrupulously careful with money, he stood out from other rich men's sons. In 1897, he graduated with the degree of Bachelor of Arts, after taking nearly a dozen courses in the social sciences. He joined the Alpha Delta Phi fraternity, and was elected to Phi Beta Kappa. After graduation, Rockefeller Jr. joined his father's business and set up operations in the newly formed family office at Standard Oil's headquarters. He became a Standard Oil director; he later also became a director in J. P. Morgan's U.S. Steel company, which had been formed in 1901.

David Rockefeller Jr. (born 1941)

David Rockefeller Jr. attended the Phillips Exeter Academy at New Hampshire and graduated from Harvard College and Harvard Law School. He settled in the Boston area and pursued his interests in music and arts education. In 1991, he was elected by his cousins to succeed his father as chairman of Rockefeller Financial Services, which is the $3 billion holding company that manages the family investments, shareholdings, and real estate. In October 2006, the Rockefeller Foundation announced the appointment of David Jr. to its board of trustees, thus becoming the sixth member of the family to have served on the board since its founding by John D. Rockefeller in 1913.

The Clintons

William Jefferson Clinton (Born 1946)

Bill Clinton attended the Edmund A. Walsh School of Foreign Service at Georgetown University in Washington, DC, receiving a Bachelor of Science in Foreign Service (BS) degree in 1968. While in college, he became a brother of Alpha Phi Omega and was elected to Phi Beta Kappa. Upon graduation, he won a Rhodes Scholarship to University College, Oxford (England), where he studied philosophy, politics, and economics, though he switched programs and left early for Yale University, and so he did not obtain a degree there. After Oxford, Clinton attended Yale Law School and obtained a Juris Doctor (JD) degree in 1973. Clinton served as governor of Arkansas (1979–81 and 1983–93). He has named two influential moments in his life that contributed to his decision to become a public figure, both occurring in 1963. One was his visit as a Boys Nation senator to the White House to meet President John F. Kennedy. The other was listening to Martin Luther King's 1963 "I Have a Dream" speech, which impressed him enough that he later memorized it. In 1992, he became the forty-second president of the United States. He was re-elected to a second term in 1996.

Hillary Rodham Clinton (Born 1947)

Hillary Rodham attended Maine East High School, where she participated in student council, the school newspaper, and was selected for National Honor Society. For her senior year, she was redistricted to Maine South High School, where she was a National Merit Finalist and graduated in the top five percent of her class of 1965. In 1965 she enrolled at Wellesley College, where she majored in political science. In 1969, she graduated with a Bachelor of Arts with departmental honors in political science. Rodham then entered Yale Law School, where she served on the editorial board of the *Yale Review of Law and Social Action*. She received a Juris Doctor degree from Yale in 1973. Following graduation, she began a year of postgraduate study on children and medicine at the Yale Child Study Center. Her early political development was shaped most by her high school history teacher (like her father, a fervent anticommunist), who introduced her to Goldwater's classic *The Conscience of a Conservative*, and by her Methodist youth minister (like her mother, concerned with issues of social justice), with whom she saw and met civil rights leader Martin Luther King Jr. in Chicago in 1962. Hillary Rodham Clinton, married to Bill Clinton, is presently the serving as the sixty-seventh United States Secretary of State.

Chelsea Clinton (Born 1980)

Chelsea attended Forest Park Elementary School, Booker Arts and Science Magnet Elementary School, and Horace Mann Junior High

School, which are public schools in Little Rock, Arkansas. She skipped the third grade. She graduated from Sidwell Friends in 1997, was a National Merit Scholarship semifinalist in 1997, and is a veteran of the Model United Nations. She entered Stanford in the fall of 1997 and graduated in 2001 with highest honors and a BA in history. In 2001, she attended the University College, Oxford (England), and was awarded an M.Phil. in international relations in 2003. She completed a Master of Public Health degree at Columbia Mailman School of Public Health, and pursued doctoral studies at the Robert F. Wagner Graduate School of Public Service, New York University. In 2003, Clinton joined the consulting firm McKinsey & Company in New York City, and went to work for Avenue Capital Group in the fall of 2006. In 2008, at the Democratic National Convention, she was quoted to say that her mother, Hillary Rodham Clinton, is '"my hero and my mother"' as she introduced her for the nomination of president of the United States. On July 31, 2010, Clinton and Marc Mezvinsky were married. Marc was a Goldman Sachs investment banker, and, at the time of the marriage, an investment banker at 3G Capital Management.

The Kennedys

In the United States, the phrase **Kennedy family** commonly refers to the family descending from the marriage of the Irish-Americans Joseph P. Kennedy Sr. and Rose Elizabeth Fitzgerald that was prominent in American politics and government. Their political involvement has revolved around the Democratic Party. Harvard University educations have been common among them, and they have contributed heavily to that university's John F. Kennedy School of Government. The wealth, glamour, and photogenic quality of the family members, as well as their extensive and continuing commitment to public service, has elevated them to iconic status over the past half-century and has led to their reputation as "America's Royal Family."

Joseph P. Kennedy Sr. (1888–1969)

Joseph Kennedy Sr., educated at Boston Latin School and Harvard University, embarked on a career in finance and made a large fortune as a stock market and commodity investor and by investing in real estate and a wide range of industries. In 1914, he married Rose Fitzgerald (1890–1995), the daughter of Boston (Massachusetts) Mayor John F. Fitzgerald. Joseph served as the first chairman of the US Securities and Exchange Commission and as the United States ambassador to the Court of St. James in the years leading up to World War II.

John Fitzgerald Kennedy (1917–1963)

John Kennedy was educated at the London School of Economics, Princeton University, and Harvard College. In 1939, Kennedy toured Europe, the Soviet Union, the Balkans, and the Middle East in preparation for his Harvard senior honors thesis. He graduated from Harvard College with a Bachelor of Science *cum laude* in international affairs in 1940. Known to his family as "Jack" and sometimes referred to as "JFK," he served as a US representative (1947–1953), a US senator (1953–1960), and the thirty-fifth US president (1961–1963). He was assassinated on November 22, 1963, while riding in a presidential motorcade in Dallas, Texas.

Eunice Mary Kennedy (1921–2009)

Eunice Mary Kennedy was educated at the Manhattanville College on the Upper West Side of Manhattan. After graduating from Stanford University with a Bachelor of Science degree in sociology in 1943, she worked for the Special War Problems Division of the US State Department. She eventually moved to the US Justice Department as executive secretary for a project dealing with juvenile delinquency. She served as a social worker at the Federal Industrial Institution for Women for one year before moving to Chicago in 1951 to work with the House of the Good Shepherd women's shelter and the Chicago Juvenile Court. She co-founded the Special Olympics in 1968, an organization she began in honor of her sister Rosemary. In 1953, she married Robert Sargent Shriver Jr. (1915–2011), who later served as the US ambassador to France in the late 1960s to early 1970s and was a 1972 vice-presidential candidate.

Robert Francis Kennedy (1925–1968)

Robert Francis Kennedy was educated at the V-12 Navy College Training Program at Harvard College in Cambridge, Massachusetts. His V-12 training was at Harvard (March–November 1944); Bates College in Lewiston, Maine (November 1944–June 1945); and Harvard (June 1945–January 1946). In September 1946, Kennedy entered Harvard as a junior, graduating from Harvard with an AB in government in March 1948. In September 1948, Kennedy enrolled at the University of Virginia School of Law and graduated in June 1951. Known as "Bob" or "Bobby" and sometimes referred to as "RFK," he served as US Attorney General (1961–1964) in his brother John's administration and later served as the junior US senator from New York (1965 to his death). He was assassinated in Los Angeles, California during his 1968 campaign for US president.

Edward Moore Kennedy (1932–2009)

Edward Kennedy was educated at Harvard where he graduated in 1956 with an AB in history and government. He enrolled in the University of Virginia School of Law in 1956, and also attended the Hague Academy of International Law during 1958. He graduated from law school in 1959 and was admitted to the Massachusetts Bar the same year. Known as "Teddy" or "Ted," he served as a US senator from Massachusetts (1962–2009). On May 20, 2008, it was announced that he had a malignant brain tumor. In the next year, brain cancer severely limited his senate appearances.

Jeff Bezos (Born 1964)

Jeff Bezos attended Miami Palmetto Senior High School in Miami, Florida. While in high school, he attended the Student Science Training Program at the University of Florida, receiving a Silver Knight Award in 1982. He attended Princeton University, planning to study physics, but soon returned to his love of computers and graduated *summa cum laude*, Phi Beta Kappa, with a Bachelor of Science in electrical engineering and computer science. Jeff worked for a short time at a hedge fund before he founded Amazon.com in 1994 after making a cross-country drive from New York to Seattle, writing up the Amazon business plan on the way. He initially set up the company in his garage. Amazon eventually made him one of the most prominent dot-com entrepreneurs and a billionaire. He was named *Time* magazine's Person of the Year in 1999. In 2008, he was selected by *U.S. News & World Report* as one of America's best leaders. Bezos was awarded an honorary doctorate in science and technology from Carnegie Mellon University in 2008.

Timothy Geithner (Born 1961)

Tim Geithner spent most of his childhood in other countries, including present-day Zimbabwe, Zambia, India, and Thailand, where he completed high school at the International School Bangkok. He attended Dartmouth College, graduating with an AB in government and Asian studies in 1983. In the process, he studied Mandarin at Peking University in 1981 and at Beijing Normal University in 1982. He earned an MA in international economics and East Asian studies from Johns Hopkins University's School of Advanced International Studies in 1985. In an unusual twist of fate, the parents of Barack Obama and Timothy Geithner shared a nonprofit connection: they worked at the Ford Foundation at the same time in the 1980s and met at least once in Jakarta. Geithner is the seventy-fifth and current United States Secretary of the Treasury, serving under President Barack Obama. He was previously the president of the Federal Reserve Bank of New York.

Henry Paulson (Born 1946)

In his early years, Henry Paulson attained the rank of Eagle Scout in the Boy Scouts of America. He received his AB in English from Dartmouth College in 1968; at Dartmouth he was a member of Phi Beta Kappa and Sigma Alpha Epsilon and he was an All-Ivy, All-East, and honorable mention All American as an offensive lineman. Paulson received his Master of Business Administration degree from Harvard Business School in 1970. He is an American banker who served as the seventy-fifth United States Secretary of the Treasury. Paulson identified the wide gap between the richest and poorest Americans as an issue on his list of the country's four major long-term economic issues to be addressed, highlighting the issue in one of his first public appearances as of Treasury. He previously served as the chairman and chief executive officer of Goldman Sachs.

James Simons (Born 1938)

James Simons was the son of a shoe factory owner in Massachusetts. He received a Bachelor of Science in mathematics from the Massachusetts Institute of Technology in 1958 and a Doctor of Philosophy, also in mathematics, from the University of California, Berkeley in 1961 at the age of twenty-three. Simons taught mathematics at the Massachusetts Institute of Technology and Harvard University. In 1968, he was appointed chairman of the math department at Stony Brook University. Simons was asked by IBM in 1973 to attack Lucifer, an early but direct precursor to DES. In 1976, he won the American Mathematical Society's Oswald Veblen Prize in Geometry. His most influential research resulted in the Chern-Simons form (Chern-Simons theory). In 1978, he left academia to run an investment fund that traded in commodities and financial instruments on a discretionary basis. He is still at the helm, as CEO, of what is now one of the world's most successful hedge funds. Simons is estimated to be worth $10.6 billion.

Henry Kravis (Born 1944)

Born the son of Raymond Kravis, Henry is a successful oil engineer who had once been a business partner of Joseph P. Kennedy. He began his education at the Eaglebrook School, 'followed by high school at the Loomis Chaffee School. He majored in economics at Claremont McKenna College in Claremont, California and graduated in 1967 before going on to Columbia Business School, where he received an MBA degree in 1969. He is the co-founder of Kohlberg Kravis Roberts & Co., a private equity firm with over $62 billion in assets as of 2011. He has an estimated net worth of $3.7 billion as of September 2011, ranked by *Forbes* as the eighty-eighth richest man in America.

David Tepper (Born 1957)

David Tepper attended the University of Pittsburgh where he paid his way through school by working at the Frick Fine Arts Library. He graduated with honors, receiving his Bachelor of Arts degree in economics. He earned his MBA from Carnegie Mellon in 1982. He is an hedge fund manager and the founder of Appaloosa Management. His investment specialty is distressed companies. In recent years he's become known as a philanthropist, his largest gift going to Carnegie Mellon University, whose Tepper School of Business is named after him. In March 2010, the *New York Times* reported that Tepper's success made him the top-earning hedge fund manager in the world in 2009, and in 2010 he was ranked by *Forbes* as the 258th richest person in the world.

Alan Dershowitz (Born 1938)

Born the son of an Orthodox Jew, Dershowitz had a strong sense of justice and talked about how it was "the Jew's job to defend the underdog." He attended Brooklyn College, receiving his AB in 1959. He attended Yale Law School, where he was editor-in-chief of the

Yale Law Journal, and graduated first in his class with a Bachelor of Laws (LLB) in 1962. An American lawyer, jurist, and political commentator, he has spent most of his career at Harvard Law School where in 1967, at the age of twenty-eight, he became the youngest full professor of law in its history. He has held the Felix Frankfurter professorship there since 1993. Dershowitz is known for his involvement in several high-profile legal cases and as a commentator on the Arab–Israeli conflict. As a criminal appellate lawyer, he has won thirteen of the fifteen murder and attempted-murder cases he has handled, and has represented a series of celebrity clients, including Mike Tyson, Patty Hearst, and Jim Bakker. His most notable cases include his role in 1984 in overturning the conviction of Claus von Bülow for the attempted murder of his wife, Sunny, and as the appellate adviser for the defense in the O.J. Simpson trial in 1995.

F. Lee Bailey (Born 1933)

Bailey received his LLB from Boston University, where he was ranked first in his graduating class in 1960. He was a criminal defense lawyer in the Sam Sheppard re-trial. He was the supervisory attorney over attorney Mark J. Kadish in the court martial of Captain Ernest Medina for the My Lai Massacre; he was the defeated lawyer in the Patty Hearst case; and was one of the lawyers for the defense in the O. J. Simpson murder case. He was disbarred for misconduct while defending Claude DuBoc. In spite of his difficulties, he still has a reputation for being a highly successful defense attorney.

Johnnie Cochran Jr. (1937-2005)

Cochran Jr. graduated first in his class from Los Angeles High School in 1955. He went on to receive his Bachelor of Science degree in business administration from the University of California, Los Angeles in 1959 and his Juris Doctor at Loyola Marymount University School of Law (now Loyola Law School) in 1962. He was a member of Kappa Alpha Psi Fraternity. He was an American lawyer best known for his leadership role in the defense and criminal acquittal of O. J. Simpson. He also represented celebrity clients Sean Combs, Michael Jackson, Tupac Shakur, Todd Bridges, Jim Brown, Snoop Dogg, Riddick Bowe, 1992 Los Angeles riot victim Reginald Oliver Denny, Geronimo Pratt, and athlete Marion Jones. Cochran was known for his skill in the courtroom and his prominence as an early advocate for victims of police brutality. Inspired by Thurgood Marshall and the legal victory he won in Brown v. Board of Education, Cochran decided to dedicate his life to practicing law. Cochran felt his career was a calling, a double opportunity to work for what he considered to be right and to challenge what he considered wrong. Despite setbacks as a lawyer, Cochran vowed not to cease what he was doing, saying, "I made this commitment and I must fulfill it."

Robert Shapiro (Born 1942)

Robert Shapiro graduated from UCLA in 1965. He obtained his Juris Doctor from Loyola Law School in 1968. He was an American civil litigator and senior partner in the Los Angeles-based law firm Glaser Weil Fink Jacobs Howard Avchen & Shapiro, LLP. Shapiro is most recognized for being part of the defense team that successfully defended O.J. Simpson in 1995. He has represented famous athletes Darryl Strawberry, José Canseco, and Vince Coleman, and celebrities such as Johnny Carson, Christian Brando, Linda Lovelace, and the Kardashians. He is the voice of, and pictured in, the television commercials for the LegalZoom company he cofounded and cofounder of Shoedazzle.com.

J. Craig Venter (Born 1946)

Venter received his BS degree in biochemistry in 1972, and his PhD degree in physiology and pharmacology in 1975, both from the University of California, San Diego. He worked as an associate professor, and later as a full professor, at the State University of

New York at Buffalo. He joined the National Institutes of Health in 1984. An American biologist and entrepreneur, he was famous for sequencing the human genome and for his role in creating the first cell with a synthetic genome in 2010. Venter founded Celera Genomics, The Institute for Genomic Research, and the J. Craig Venter Institute, now working at the latter to create synthetic biological organisms and to document genetic diversity in the world's oceans. He was listed on *Time* magazine's 2007 and 2008 lists of the one hundred most influential people in the world. In 2010, the British magazine *New Statesman* listed Craig Venter at fourteenth in its list of "The World's 50 Most Influential Figures."

Warren Buffet (Born 1930)

Born the son of US representative Howard Buffett, Warren Buffet was educated at the Wharton Business School of the University of Pennsylvania from 1947 to 1949. In 1950, at age nineteen, he transferred to the University of Nebraska–Lincoln , where he graduated with a Bachelor of Science in business administration. He earned a Master of Science in economics from Columbia Business School in 1951. An American business magnate, investor, and philanthropist, he is one of the most successful investors in the world. He is the primary shareholder, chairman, and CEO of Berkshire Hathaway. He is consistently ranked among the world's wealthiest people. He was ranked as the world's wealthiest person in 2008 and is the third wealthiest person in the world as of 2011.

What does Warren Buffet have in common with the rest of the people on this list? What do they all have in common—besides being 10 percent income earners? You may have noticed that all the people on our list have post-graduate education, have a mentor or someone who influenced their lives, have great ambition, and are professionals. You've counted eleven lawyers, two doctors, nine business people, four public servants, one educator, and one financier.

But what is it that really that makes these individuals special? Earning money isn't what makes them different, because money is only a symptom of a positive attitude, pursuit of worthy goals, and making intelligent decisions. Wealthy people not only live differently, but they also *think* differently.

An article on the website Way-of-the-Mind.com titled "Rich People: What Do They Have in Common?" (August 2009) compiled a list of basic qualities the rich seem to share. These qualities can be found in many wealthy people:

--They refuse to be overwhelmed by the challenges of life. They know that what we concentrate on grows, so they concentrate on opportunities, not obstacles.

--Once they have decided to do something, they start acting right away. They make a commitment, when 90 percent of us are contented with wishful thinking.

--They take action instead of being busy. We all have twenty-four hours per day. The rich make sure they are making good use of their time. They don't waste time in activities that lead nowhere.

--They take responsibility for what they do, instead of believing the world owes them anything. Rich people know the difference between responsibility and entitlement.

--They understand that the fact that one person getting richer doesn't make others poorer. Being rich is not like a lottery with only one winner. So, instead of resenting other rich people, they admire them.

--The main occupation they select fully capitalizes on their abilities.

--While they usually excel in one area, they have multiple sources of income, many of them being passive income.

--They are interested in many things, but focus on one at a time. This is a great recipe for success allowing them to take one thing at a time instead of spreading themselves thin. This way, they can accomplish a lot more.

--They think big. They think long term. They know the amount of effort applied at the onset is not proportional to the results. So they look for the maximum reward for the same effort.

--When they are negotiating, they are aggressive. They are willing to walk away from the deal at any time. They are not afraid to lose. If they lose, they have enough energy and commitment to rebuild what they have lost.

--They believe in basic success factors such as integrity, discipline, relationships, hard work, career enjoyment, and leadership skills.

--They reduce their worries with preparation, focus, and decisiveness.

--They usually choose a supportive spouse who complements their goals.

--They often have strong spiritual beliefs.

This is the way that winners think. If you want to be a winner, you'll have to think like one, but it's not always comfortable. Ninety percent of us stray from this way of thinking because it's easier to be lazy and self-centered, and to avoid taking responsibility. Being average is easy.

What's not easy is achieving greatness, but it's more than possible.

Chapter 3
The College Myth

We believe you should focus on financial success early on in life, and your career path is an important consideration.

You've probably noticed that it's a popular trend that the career plans of many have not panned out as promised. How many people do you know who are not working in the field that they majored in, or are not as successful as they thought they would be?

In fact, we subscribe to the belief that most of Americans' career plans have fallen short of expectations or have fallen completely off a cliff.

That simply means that those people are not living the lifestyle they planned and their career dreams did not come true.

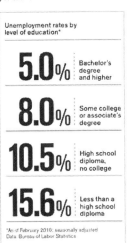

Employability: The more educated you are, the less likely you are to be out of work.

Unemployment rates by level of education*

5.0% Bachelor's degree and higher

8.0% Some college or associate's degree

10.5% High school diploma, no college

15.6% Less than a high school diploma

*As of February 2010; seasonally adjusted
Data: Bureau of Labor Statistics

Our focus is to do better than this group that poorly planned their future.

The table to the left (Kalwarski, n.d.) supports the traditional belief that having a college degree equals employment.

This table only shows unemployment and doesn't compare the income and benefit levels of those with degrees.

These numbers are a bit misleading and are the basis of the college myth. If you look at these numbers alone, you might think that going to college is a good bet and then ignore any additional considerations. Yet there are many in the 90 percent who went to college and completed a degree program, and now find themselves underpaid, underemployed, or unemployed.

Embedded in the theory of Optimal Career Planning is the premise that most of the career choices and execution of the currently disappointed was flawed in some way, or don't fit today's reality.

Now I am not blaming anyone—in fact, I am quite sure most people did exactly what they thought they should do. Their path was based on the spectrum of possibilities from following conventional wisdom to complying with the advice of the "experts" who pushed that getting a college degree was simply enough. This is painfully true in the case of very recent graduates; the classes of 2008 – 2011.

I will address typical career planning options and point out why they are no longer successful in today's economic environment. As you might expect, I will relate these flawed plans back to my underlying premise that they failed to advance the individual into the security of financial and career independence.

The Lights Are On But Is Anybody Home?

These observations are not meant to insult anyone. Much of what I am recommending is based on hard work—hard work planning, hard work studying, hard work saving, and so on. And I'm not saying people don't work hard, but maybe they're not working hard enough, and may-be they're working at the wrong things. My observations reveal that when it comes to a goal like reaching career and financial independence, most don't start with a plan, or the plan is flawed, or they don't work hard or smart enough on a plan that can deliver the goods.

You heard me mention the "College and Pray Plan." This is a plan—not very directed, not very specific, with no back up by anything tangible—filled with good intentions: Parents save money for college, send out applications to appropriate institutions, maybe visit a few universities with their children, and choose from those colleges offering acceptance. They pack up their child, send him or her off to school, stir in some spending money, and wait for a newly minted college graduate to come out on the other end. If all goes well, a college graduate is produced, a lucrative career ensues, and all's well that ends well.

Not these days. I know now that this is the exception and not the rule in today's economic and employment market (Wolverson, Time Business, May 2011). Even if employment is the result, for most, dissatisfaction, pay cuts, and layoffs loom as a regular occurrence or possibility.

Of course there are myriad variations of the "College and Pray Plan." I propose that this is really no plan, and falls far short of what is needed to reach the top in today's world.

"Do What You Love" Myth

This is one of my favorite flawed career advice phrases. Yet various forms of this philosophy still permeate almost all of the rhetoric contained in career planning publications, career counselor assessments, and online consultant advice.

It's hard even for us to counter such a widely used premise as it makes us, and obviously others, feel so good. As a result it attracts many, not unlike a box full of puppies. And to be fair, in the past this centerpiece of career planning may have worked out for those who followed its warm sentiment, but that was a relatively long time ago, and in what now seems like a land far, far away.

In discussions with career counselors regarding my own kids, the "do what you love" premise is their default position. After quizzing the counselors about lucrative career paths, financial and career independence, and ways to achieve such results, I asked about choosing such a path *for* my children. After the shocked looks and raised eyebrows waned, I was summarily warned that I cannot "push" my kids into any particular career. Doing so would be at our peril. It was reasoned that if they don't love what they do, they won't stick with it, or if they do, they will be miserable. I didn't have the heart to ask if these kids would feel equally miserable being either unemployed or unable to earn a proper living.

Online career coaching and advice websites follow similar unrealistic "feel good" recommendations. Although they are apt to discuss the most lucrative and employable career choices, in the end they fall back to counseling or surveys that purportedly predict a career path that will end up being "loved" by its pursuer. Little or no time is spent relating such a choice to lifestyle, job security, or financial goals. They continue to cling to the notion that if you "do what you love," everything works out, or at least it always used to.

"Smart Student = High Paying Job" Myth

Aptitude tests and surveys don't guarantee, or even assure, that financial and career independence will be reached. I know—this is in direct conflict to conventional wisdom. Furthermore, these instruments do not bother to consider what it takes to reach the important "higher" levels of wealth creation. And maybe that's not their job, but all too often the results of these tests are trusted to imply financial success. The National Center for Education Statistics (NCES) estimates that over 1.78 million students will graduate with a bachelor's degree in 2012, with 66% holding an average of $23,200 in student debt. The average amount of debt held by a graduate student is significantly higher, closer to $100,000.

Numerous examples of aptitude tests populate the Internet, bookstores, and the quivers of career counselors and coaches. Their premise is noble and they are trusted and relied upon for the following reasons. It is posited that if you choose an educational path that fits your aptitude or personality you will:

- Get better grades

- Pick a college major and not change it
- Complete your college education in the expected four years
- Enjoy more career satisfaction and success

The purveyors of these assessment tools attempt to offer proof that such results have worked time and time again, and will continue to deliver. But in today's economic reality I have found that these results are not guaranteed, and are at the very least naïve. When it comes to planning for career and financial independence, this basis for career selection is woefully out of touch. Let's address each of the tenets above, but in reverse order.

People who have followed the results of these assessments and this inadequate career planning advice are now finding themselves underemployed, unemployed, or working outside of their specialty. I cannot define that as career satisfaction or success. I have personal experience with many who used this college planning method and had a period of success, yet they are now unemployed. Such approaches are not appropriate for today when there is a glut of college graduates and a business climate where "head count" reduction is the way to increase profits.(Marcelino, April, 2012)

Today, college degrees often take longer to complete than the old "rule of thumb" would have you believe, which is four years. This has much to do with the schedule of which classes are offered by the institutions and the revenue generated by lengthy college stays. It is also due to a lack of optimizing, planning, and monitoring exactly how many credit hours are completed by a student each semester. The fact is, when college takes longer, it has little to do with one's aptitude and more to do with one's work ethic, planning, and a commitment to that plan, in addition to the universities' class availability.

Picking a college major and sticking with it certainly can be partially correlated to one's interests and personality. I personally would question sticking with something that will only lead to a life of worry. I'm sure you've heard of students changing their major midway through college because the job prospects of their first choice were poor.

My goal is for your child to be independent of market forces that can at any time cause a pay cut or layoff or force him or her to work in a position or profession that has nothing to do with the vocation for which he or she has aptitude. Since my premise is financial independence, I find it unproductive to pursue a college major based solely on aptitude. To grossly exaggerate this fallacy, if your child is excellent at the clarinet, then they should major in music and everything else will fall into place after their graduation, right? Practical factors and historically successful career choices must be considered.

Getting good grades is steeped in a solid work ethic, native ability, and the routine practice of meeting high expectations. We have all had to take courses throughout our educations that we didn't "like." What we end up liking is also influenced by our environment, our various mentors, early training, and developmental experiences. Specific preparation during our formative years is critical. Such preparation should include acquiring a solid work ethic, realizing "good grades," and achieving at a higher level than our peers. These attributes must become independent of our aptitude. Academic performance must be viewed as a means to an end, and not a result of what we are apt to "like."

"It's Always Been Done this Way" Myth

Throw out the old playbook and the old rules of college planning; it's for the best. Today's economic realities demand it. And it takes time, effort, and commitment to redirect our view of career planning, but it's necessary and worth it. Earning power is important to live the lifestyle you want, but you must also consider the rising cost of college, and the future struggle of getting out of debt. - Glenn Harlan Reynolds in his recently published book "The Higher Education Bubble", examines the math of a college investment. College tuitions vastly outpace inflation and family incomes. Going to college, hoping, doing what you love, and relying on traditional career planning advice no longer makes the grade. Especially if you want to make sure your child does not have to suffer the insecurity of a typical college graduate. The "old" ways have got to go. Optimal Career Planning is a program that provides a better way.

Chapter 4
"Warning: Optimal Career Planning Isn't For Everyone"

"Whenever you find yourself on the side of the majority, it is time to pause and reflect." –Mark Twain

Greatness is possible. There are students who have gone directly from college (Goudreau, 2012) and become business executives or they have been so far ahead of everyone else they were working well before their college age (Roberts, 2012).

We want to offer you this caveat so that you fully understand the commitment required for the Optimal Career Planning program to work for you. It's statistically probable that you won't take the full advice of this book and you may even openly disagree with our logic. It doesn't really matter what you do with the information we offer, yet I do want to provide fair warning as Optimal Career Planning takes a number of attributes in order to execute.

For some, what's required will be a significant shift in mindset and behavioral patterns. For others who already pursue career goals in alignment with my philosophy, only minor adjustments may need to be made. In the case of a parent(s) and child team, all will have to be committed to the program and its components for the long term.

It might be more helpful to view Optimal Career Planning as adopting a particular career "lifestyle." When habits that lead to desired results are formed, the practice becomes second nature. In that our goal is to launch you and/or your child into the top 10 percent of wage earners, we have studied the habits and career development of those who earn at that level. As a result we have extracted those commonalities and incorporated them into our program.

At the risk of stating the obvious, if any of these behaviors is missing from your student's normal practice, we will be asking you to adopt them. Once these become natural, you are well on your way to our suggested mindset and career development "lifestyle."

This program is not for everyone: if you're unwilling or unable to change for the sake of eliminating career and financial worry, this program is not for you. However, exposing yourself to our material certainly can't hurt, and may provoke you into considering our findings and recommendations.

Here, we address the basics of Optimal Career Planning. Later chapters will address each component of the program in detail.

The Formula:

Smart Work + Native Ability + Power Alley(s) + Luck = Financial Independence

Certainly some of the variables in "the formula" are familiar to you; others may be new. What is unique is their combination and our interpretation of each one. What follows is your first introduction to these critical components.

Smart Work: Notice we didn't use the term "hard work." But make no mistake, Smart Work is hard work—very hard work. It's just more directed. You've probably heard the phrase, "'You've got to work smarter, not harder." Working hard is noble, but working hard at something that is not based in a proven, logical pursuit of success is wasted energy.

Native Ability: "What 'you're good at" or one's inherent or natural ability to do things is an important factor in succeeding at the highest level. Applied to a person, "ability" might be considered the same as "capacity," but they are different.

Power Alley: A Power Alley is a career path that has historically led to financial independence. A Power Alley can be a specific profession or a combination of acquired skill sets that synergize one's professional value.

Luck: Yes, luck! It exists and we know that all those people who are financially independent and secure in their careers would admit they had some luck along the way. I will address the concept of luck, but only within the context of minimizing its influence.

In order to build upon "The Formula" and the pathways it sets out to offer, you will require a solid foundation. The following are principles that we have discovered are preferable, and actually necessary, to provide the highest predictable success. If you and your student have these foundations, or are willing to acquire them, then executing the Optimal Career Planning program becomes no more difficult than following a recipe.

Foundations for Parents

- Belief that a career which provides financial independence is worth total commitment.
- Able to create a trusted, interactive relationship with their child.
- High expectations for their child's education and performance.
- Able to set an example that equals the expectations for their child.
- Influence the environment and individuals that surround their child.
- Possess a continuous thirst for wisdom, knowledge, and self-improvement.
- Provides wide and rich experiences that support their child's development.
- Able to establish and follow a plan over the long term.

Foundations for Students
- Exhibits native ability to learn, focus, and follow a plan.

- Enjoys engaging people, the world, and new things.
- Strives to do well in school, hobbies, and personal relationships.
- Has a vision for the future.
- Chooses healthy associations and relationships.
- Is decisive and has a record of making good choices.

So as you can see, there is a specific set of attributes that will be required by the parent/child team.

We also believe that all of these attributes are attainable, and can be cultivated and developed. If you and your child already possess some or all of the "foundations," then we congratulate you. If you have some work to do in order to round out what is needed, we are here to help you. If you're the parent of a younger child, consider yourself lucky—you now have the time and the roadmap to develop what we all can agree are desired personal characteristics.

We do not set out to claim that this will be necessarily easy. I do think that if you adapt these plans and goals as a "lifestyle," it won't seem quite so "hard." What we can assure you, whatever the career outcome, is that every effort you make toward adopting our philosophy and career planning advice can only provide benefits for all of life's pursuits.

Chapter 5
The Power Alleys: End Games that Work!

"Mamas, don't let your babies grow up to be cowboys
Don't let 'em pick guitars and drive them old trucks
Make 'em be doctors and lawyers and such" – Willie Nelson

SMART WORK + NATIVE ABILITY + POWER ALLEY(S) + LUCK = FINANCIAL INDEPENDENCE

As we've discussed previously, some of the components in this formula are familiar, and some are not.

We will explain all of the variables in the formula, but for now our discussion will focus on the one that may seem the most unfamiliar.

Power Alleys

Power Alleys are those vocations and career pursuits that year after year and generation after generation land people in the top 10 percent of wage earners.

We want you to fully grasp the big picture of what we're sharing with you. Think back now—you're already in the know regarding the concentration of wealth. We've helped you realize that the only way to become career and financially independent is to get as close to, if not directly into, the top 10 percent segment of the wealth distribution.

We provided examples of those individuals and legacy families who perennially occupy this upper end segment of the financially able. That effort was undertaken in order to study the commonalities among the members of this group. Upon our review, and probably yours as well, we find a few degree and career pursuits that have consistently generated superior outcomes—professions that, generation after generation, deliver practitioners to the top 10 percent.

We call these pursuits the Power Alleys. They are:

* Medicine (medical doctor, scientist)
* Finance (accountant, investment banker, financial advisor, investment manager, venture capitalist)
* The Law (lawyer)
* Executive Management (non-finance)

It's a very short list, isn't it? One might even consider it limiting, or in no way representative of all those people you consider successful. Today's education experts would argue that STEM (science, technology, engineering, and math) subjects are the best for future employment potential, which is true, and that's why there's some overlap. However, all of the careers available to those who study in the STEM fields are not exactly power alleys because they simply don't have the same potential for earning power.

Did you know that out of the "Forbes 400" (the four hundred richest people in America), five studied medicine, twenty-six are PhDs, thirty-five studied law, and one hundred nine have master's degrees (with eighty-four of those having MBAs)? In this select list, the Power Alleys are well represented.

We're aware that there are many success stories from every vocation pursued in our great land. But we are not here to guide you to a rare occurrence, nor am I here to dissuade anyone from embarking on a career path he or she believes to be worthy. We are also aware of those (like fellow education activist Dale J. Stephens, who runs uncollege.org, a website that offers alternatives to school and tips for "career hacking") who challenge the notion that college is the only avenue for success.

What we'd like to get you thinking about is those vocations that, based on research going back to 1979, (US Office of Tax Analysis, 2009) have not failed to produce upper-end incomes. And as a result of this historical consistency, we know that those who have succeeded in these specific pathways have also enjoyed career and financial independence.

Now before you say to yourself, "Still too limiting; I don't buy it," consider the truth that college is really an investment. Good investments require a successful track record, careful planning, and research into their future stability.

In an effort to make these successful career pursuits more versatile, we will offer variations on the Power Alleys and mash-ups with alternative areas of study later in this chapter.

We will also introduce other enhancements and the concept of synergies that further widen the possibilities for you and your child. But humor me for now, and let's keep our current discussion focused on the big four Power Alleys.

The chart below is an excerpt from "Jobs and Income of Top Earners and the Causes of Changing Income Inequality: Evidence from US Tax Return Data" by Bakija, Cole, and Heim, which shows current data regarding the vocations of those in the top 1 percent.

Figure 3. Percentage of Tax Payers in Top 1 Percent of Income Distribution

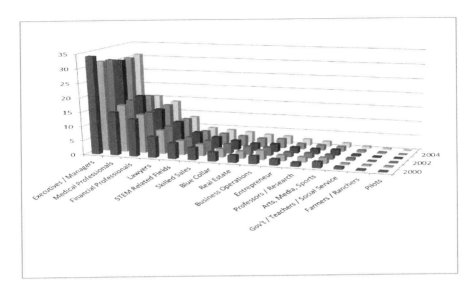

As you study this information it will become extremely clear why our focus is on these four Power Alleys.

As you can see, the data is clear. Whether you look back ten, twenty, or thirty years, or just concentrate on the facts of today, a career in medicine, finance, the law, or executive management can take one to the top of the income mountain. As a result we see no reason why one would not want to prepare for a career in one of the Power Alleys, at least as a foundation.

There is a story, which may or may not be true, about President John Adams. But it illustrates our point very clearly. One day President Adams' son, John Quincy Adams, came to him to discuss his life interests. John Quincy Adams said to his father, "Father, when I grow up I am going to be a farmer." John Adams, after briefly contemplating his son's statement, replied, "Son, farming is a very noble profession, and the world needs many good farmers. But you, my son, will be studying the law." I bet you don't have to guess what John Quincy Adams studied in school.

Anthony Meister, co-author of this book, recalls that not unlike John Adams, the genesis for this program originated out of concern for his daughter. He wanted her to have an understanding of what it will take for her to become career and financially independent.

When I began to believe my research and concepts wholeheartedly, it was time to introduce the concepts to her. Luckily, and much by accident, I had been laying down many of the foundations for her academic and life success. Luckier still, she has native ability and has always done well in school. When I approached her with the Power Alley concept, none of those options had occurred to her, nor did they appear to be of any immediate interest.

In relatively small doses I explained this program to her, why I am promoting it, and why I believe it's in her best interest to consider it. Again, I'm lucky—my daughter is an observer of her surroundings, sees the financial pressures on her mother, father, and her friends' parents. She has also observed others in who do not have financial difficulties. Given the contrasts, she easily came to conclusion she would like no part of the typical financial struggles in the world today, and she agreed to research and explore areas of study and careers that would position her for top-tier earning potential.

What happened over the next several weeks as we discussed the realities of the current economy can only be considered teenage enlightenment. Working backward from how she foresees her life as an adult, we roughed in a calculation of how much she would need to earn annually. In order to realize such a goal and beyond, it became clear to her which careers would coincide with her lifestyle desires. With her uncle serving as an example—he is a successful finance professional—my daughter agreed to gear her high school curriculum toward a career in finance.

I tell you this story in order to make this crucial point. Anyone can adopt, borrow, and practice the concepts presented in The College Unicorn. *I'm not bragging—those things my family and I have done in order to make my daughter a good person, we came by naturally. Her intellect and native ability are not the result of specialized parenting or some private school. "We"—or should I say "she"— got lucky; we discovered the secrets of the financial elite and adopted* The College Unicorn *mindset before it was too late. The transformation for my family out of middle class to financial independence begins with my daughter.*

Researching the Power Alleys

Researching the Power Alleys is up to you. Much research on each specialization can be found in books, on the Internet, or by interviewing successful practitioners. Simply by searching Monster.com or CareerBuilder.com for "dentist" you will find prospective jobs, job descriptions, and requirements. The search "I want to be a dentist" in google.com yielded many search results. In addition, by searching Amazon.com, you will find a large number of books on how to become a lawyer, doctor, or finance professional. We encourage you, with your children, to do all of the above prior to college, rather than after the fact.

Executive Management

The fourth power alley is executive management. This career pursuit is much less specific than the three power alleys of medicine, finance, and the law, and thus we need to elaborate on the subject. Interestingly, a background in a business-related Power Alley like Finance or Law is an excellent pedigree for an aspiring executive manager.

For example: Waste Management chairman and CEO David Steiner was Waste Management's general counsel and chief financial officer before getting the top job.

Jeff Smisek, chairman and CEO of United Continental Airlines, has an undergraduate degree in economics and a Harvard Law degree.

Doug Oberhelman, chairman and CEO of Caterpillar, started in the company's finance department and served as chief financial officer (CFO) before becoming CEO. He has a bachelor's degree in finance. Not surprisingly, the man who Oberhelman replaced as CEO, Jim Owens, had a PhD in economics. If you'll notice, the power alleys are represented in the education backgrounds of these gentlemen who are on the top of the corporate ladder.

So how do we define executive management? First, let's turn to the indispensable Wikipedia, which defines it as: In business, the executive officers are the top officers of a corporation, the chief executive officer (CEO) being the best-known type. The definition varies; for instance, the California Corporate Disclosure Act defines "executive officers" as the five most highly-compensated officers not also sitting on the board of directors. In many insurance policies, executive officer means, in the case of a corporation, any chairman, chief executive officer, chief financial officer, chief operating officer, president, or general counsel. In the case of a sole proprietorship, an executive officer is the sole proprietor. In the case of a partnership, an executive officer is a managing partner, senior partner, or administrative partner. In the case of a limited liability company, an executive officer is any member, manager, or officer.

We define executive management a little differently. We use two tests to determine if an employee is an executive:

1. The employee is privy to confidential financial, strategic, personnel, and planning information in an organization.
2. The employee is provided by the corporation with wealth-building benefits not provided to others in the organization. Such benefits include stock grants, stock options, phantom stock, bonus structures, annual and long-term incentive pay, severance packages in case of dismissal, special health insurance, and other perquisites like company subsidized loans, automobiles, and use of the corporate jet. These are

some of the perks 'companies feel they need to retain top talent at the executive level.

Let us flush this two-part test out with a real-world example. So we don't infringe on any copyrights we point you to http://www.executiveemploymentagreements.com where in the lower right-hand corner you can view former vice president Dick Cheney's employment agreement.

At Halliburton, Dick Cheney's position in the employment agreement passes the two tests:

1. He is privy to important corporate strategy and financial performance information, and
2. He receives special wealth-compounding perquisites.

The routes and strategies used by successful executive managers can be recounted by an Internet search directed at these individuals and various books dedicated to the pursuit of managerial greatness and excellence in business. All of the concepts and practices we advise in the Power Alleys can be supported with real-world examples.

As mentioned early on in *The College Unicorn*, we want better outcomes for our children than what we've experienced ourselves. So let's put a personal face on our examples, as coauthor Anthony Meister recounts his own career history.

As you know, my involvement in this book stemmed from wanting a more secure future for my children than I was able to achieve for myself. My experience will help you avoid certain mistakes based on my own trial and error (another poor career strategy). Although I hadn't yet formed the concept of the Power Alleys, I intuitively and experientially knew for me, executive management was my path. Moreover, I was not a doctor, lawyer, or finance professional.

Since there was no The College Unicorn *at the time, my career strategy embodied the "college and pray" plan. My parents had saved to pay for my education, got me into a state university, and it was up to me. By twists and turns of fate and some native ability in science and math, I ended up completing a degree in civil engineering. Conventional career advice would tout engineering as a preferred career path, and that course of study has allowed me to make living, but only to a point. The following career phase summaries are a brief accounting of my work history and my unstructured attempts to reach the level of management executive.*

Career Phase 1 (Age 27 to 35)

After working my way through a number of construction and contracting assignments after college that utilized my engineering training, I had established myself as a competent project manager. I had designed and overseen the building of highways, bridges, and buildings. Early job experiences exposed me to those executive managers who seemed to have a certain calm and confidence, that I now know only skill, reputation, and career and financial independence brings.

Environmental remediation contractors were all the rage in the 1980s. In 1987, I landed a job within a growing environmental contracting firm, in San Francisco, California. As my tenure grew at this up-and-coming firm, I had proven myself as a top contributor to the bottom line, and was a trusted friend of the CEO and others in top management. After three years of solid service as a project manager, I was promoted to division manager. Mind you, this was not an executive management position; it was a middle management position with lots of pressure and average compensation, but it certainly was the next step toward my goal. My theory, based on nothing other than my own perception and faith, was to work hard, continue to produce, and with my close relationships in top management, I would eventually be promoted to executive management.

Five years later, after executing my theory of hard work and production, offers to move up never came. At the time I had no idea why, but looking back I believe that so many others were in line for upper management (who had more experience and tenure) that I probably didn't even appear on the "radar" for consideration. In fact, that's most likely why the prospect of my moving up was never discussed. Even raises in salary were infrequent, but long hours (and pressure-packed meetings that were called when profits weren't as expected) became more and more common. After a number of poor acquisitions threatened the financial health of the company, it was time for me to move on.

In Career Phase 1, I learned that long-term dedication and high performance guarantee nothing. Even upper-level relationships are not an entry to executive management. I also learned, in distant retrospect, that no one is going to plan career advancement for you; action must be taken on your own. In this case, a direct inquiry should have been made regarding advancement, salary increases, and a "road map" to top management. Moving on much earlier would have wasted less time once I had discovered that such an opportunity was never in their plan for me.

Career Phase 2 (Age 35 to 39)

In an effort to leverage my environmental contracting experience, I set my sights on well-established environmental companies, the goal was to land a position with a Fortune 500 firm. I naively thought that would lead me to an executive management position.

A reconnection with my network provided just such an opportunity. A college friend was the division manager of a Fortune 500 environmental firm. He was open to exploring possibilities within that firm on my behalf. After some intermittent contact he offered me a project management position working for him. The opportunity looked excellent, and once again I had a relationship with someone at the top of the business unit in which I would work. This seemed to be fertile ground for advancement to an executive position. Bringing my philosophy of hard work and top performance to the position, it was not long before I was considered a valued member of the operation. We built a highly successful team that generated business growth, customer service excellence, and year-over-year profit increases.

Riding high on the momentum of continued successes, I settled into my role and became confident that my contributions would be noticed and advancement would be the reward. My appetite for entry into the executive level was fueled by added observations of those who occupied such positions within this firm. Even the division manager level, which my friend enjoyed, provided salary levels and bonuses that would accrue financial independence over a lifetime. Others at levels above division leadership demonstrated the confidence that comes when financial worries disappear. I thought I was in a position once again to be promoted executive management.

Unfortunately, outside forces are impossible to predict...or maybe not if you are a student of them, but I did not study such forces, and therefore was in for a surprise. The surprise came in the form of a corporate merger. Within months of the "deal" being finalized, rumors of headcount reduction permeated the company. Unfortunately the rumors were correct, and all management positions from division manager on down, including me, were dismissed in favor of a management team coming in from the new parent company. But those above the division manager level, the "executives," remained in their positions, or were offered alternative roles somewhere else in the "new" organization. This is why I believe achieving executive management status is so important.

Once again I would be starting over, and this time not by choice. Even more damaging, after the merger chaos settled, my friend and division manager was pursued legally for confidentiality and financial infractions. Years later I would find out that my mere association with this division and my division manager had damaged my reputation within this company, making further employment with this firm impossible.

In this career phase I learned that outside forces (economic conditions, stockholder pressure, corporate level decision making, etc.) can derail any career plan, especially for those below the executive level. I also learned that one has to be a student of his or her respective industry to see these things coming. Focusing on educational advancement and professional credentials build one's personal brand, and such a focus adds value and career security. And, finally, be a consistent observer of those around you. Associations with unscrupulous people can have ill career effects not only in the short term, but for the rest of your career.

Career Phase 3 (Ages 39 to 50)

In what was a reaction to my recent distaste for what can be the impersonal nature of very large corporations, the focus for my next career iteration was on small to medium-sized companies. I was also interested in change outside the environmental arena, as I had been in this business for the past twelve years. With my network unable to provide the next opportunity, I turned to a "cold calling" campaign aimed at the submission of multiple applications and resumes targeted at desirable firms. After a couple of months of diligent pursuit, I was contacted by an engineering consulting firm, that was looking for an operations manager. The company, the work, and the seemingly high interest in learning from me, made my decision easy.

I was now at a firm that employed the best and the brightest in its field, and worked with a leadership team who repeatedly confirmed they were interested in my ideas and advancement. This particular consulting service occupied a very unique niche, one that was said to be insulated from any volatility in the economy. As I learned the business and became an integral participant, the business grew rapidly, so much so we were turning some clients away. This produced generous profits and income for top management. With such direct access to the consultant/owners and the executive managers, along with my ability to work hard and perform at a high level, I was sure I would become an executive at this firm. This situation put me as close as I had ever been to a group of those who've accessed a level of income and annuities that truly define career and financial independence.

As one ages, time seems to pass more quickly...one can get caught up in raising children and pursuing other interests, and that's what happened to me. Even though I had lost confidence in the existing leadership, was treated poorly by the CEO and COO, and was generally miserable at the five-year mark, I ignored these "red flags." As a result, years went by, and I became more proficient in my operations role and my contributions to the company continued. But no real offer, or discussion, came regarding an opportunity for me to join the ranks of the senior executive team. Another sign of executive inclusion was the award of common stock. Many around me with less tenure, and some located below me on the organizational chart, were offered this form of ownership, but not me. It became clear that the consultant/owners had no plans for me...neither to move up nor to become an owner of the company. But my mastery of the work and annual raises and bonuses kept me complacent and steady in my "rut."

As a result, a decade passed, and we arrived in the recessionary times with which we continue to be challenged. It turns out this "recession-proof" business was heavily leveraged to the domestic auto industry. When the American automakers went all but bankrupt, they suspended purchasing services from my firm and revenues plummeted by 30 percent. Frustrated by the financial downturn at the company, and with no plan forward, the consultant/owners relieved the executive managers of their positions. Of course, these executives were highly rewarded over time, and at the end, for their participation. After this transition, the new chief executive officer (one of the consultant/owners) expressed how much he valued me, and the fact that he looked forward to my leadership in the new regime. It looked like my breakthrough into executive management would finally occur.

My firm's recovery from this loss of business would be slow, headcount reductions would continue, and a general sense of nervousness existed throughout the organization. Rumors circled about others who would be sacrificed, but all of my coworkers assured me I was invaluable. Then one Tuesday morning I was contacted by the new chief operating officer and was asked to attend a meeting later that day. When you've been around as long as I have, you can predict the agenda of certain meetings based solely on the attendees. As I entered the room I noted the HR manager, the new chief operating officer, and the newly appointed deputy CEO. This certainly did not look good. You see, my biggest fan and supporter, the current CEO, was on a month's vacation out of the country. As I'm sure you've concluded by now, this meeting was to reduce headcount by one more, and that head would be mine. My eleven-year "career" at this firm would culminate with being allowed to gather a few essentials from my office and an escorted walk to the back door of the facility.

Unfortunately, I fell prey to my complacency once again: working hard, contributing to the organization, ignoring the "red flags," and thinking that those at the top will eventually invite you to join their club. Such expectations, it turns out, are those of a fool. If I had "-listened"- to my misery, and began seeking a new opportunity, I might have improved my chances at an executive position elsewhere. Had I spent all that time improving my personal brand through gaining additional education and credentials, I'd have been more attractive to my current employer or some other firm. It pains me to tell you that a peer at this firm acquired an MBA, essentially on company time, and is now the chief operating officer.

Unfortunately, my story is not unique. In this day and age you can hear about others with similar experiences in as many articles or programs as you care to view. What is unique is that I never want my kids to be able to tell a similar story, and I don't want yours to either. I wanted to do something about it. As a result I've read, researched, and coauthored *The College Unicorn* for the benefit of my daughter. I want her to learn from my experience, and I want to sound the alarm for parents and their children that picking just any college major and employing sub-optimal career strategies are no longer viable when career and financial independence is the goal.

There are many things we can learn from our coauthor's story and experiences. These lessons can help one better execute a plan and entry into executive management. They can also help in a more general way, as they are good practices for those pursuing any of the Power Alleys. As you reflect upon Anthony's story, you will no doubt come up with things he could have done, and things you should do. But we shall endeavor to extract a number of ideas we feel are important for you to take away when it comes to helping your children make a career plan.

What follows is a summary of important teachings that we advise for a college and career plan that leads to executive management and can also be applied to the other Power Alleys. These lessons are also important components of a career plan that results in financial independence.

- The "college and pray plan" should not become the "career hope" plan. We use the phrase "the top 10 percent" a lot in this book. Each day one should aim to be the in the top 10 percent of those in their field, regardless of what that field is. If that means getting an advanced degree, delivering above and beyond expectations, presenting innovative ideas to boost the bottom line, thinking strategically about their customers, company, and industry, so be it.

- Hard work and top performance guarantee nothing. Expecting to reach career and financial independence through simply "doing a good job" is futile. First of all, doing a good job is not enough. It takes the right attitude, training, effort, environment, organization, and colleagues to excel in any career, let alone reach a position in executive management.

- Any career plan outside of the Power Alleys should be combined with another skill or degree in order to create a Skill Set Synergy. Our coauthor received a degree in engineering, but that alone was not value-added enough to facilitate entry into executive management. For example, a deep understanding of finance, the law, or proficiency in a foreign language would have made him more valuable to his various employers.

- Acquiring value-added training and achievements should be a life-long pursuit. We advise striving for all qualifications and skills possible from childhood to college graduation. But accomplishments after college graduation must include a plan to acquire advanced degrees, certifications, licenses, and skills. This keeps one valuable, relevant, and shows drive and determination.

- Relationships can be an incredible asset, but are to be managed in a way they doesn't become a detriment. We advocate learning to build lasting friendships and a reputable network of contacts from cradle to grave. Your friends and colleagues, with their own reputations for excellence, will be the best source of future opportunities. But re-evaluation of one's relationships must also be continuous. A toxic connection or a disingenuous peer or boss can harm prospects and waste years.

- Study your industry and not just your job. Being very accomplished at your role within an organization is certainly a priority, but being a student of your particular industry, your organization, and how these things relate to the economy in general and your organization's position in the marketplace forces you to think strategically, like an executive.

Management's actions speak louder than words. Anthony learned that his superiors told him that he was vital and important to the organization, but did they implement his strategies? Did they offer him executive compensation packages? Could he pass the two tests, as we define executive management? That leads us to…

- Blind faith and unsubstantiated trust have no place in your career, and for that matter, in your life. As President Ronald Reagan once said, "Trust but verify. " Living your career and your life with the belief that tomorrow will be as good as, or better than today, is pure folly. Plowing away at a college curriculum or in a job expecting success based only on hope is illogical. Execute your own plan based on facts and research. When goals aren't met after significant time and effort, it's probably time for re-evaluation and a change in either your strategy, your firm, or both.

A career in the executive management Power Alley is a challenging and rewarding path. Our guidance would suggest that , if interested in this path, your student structure a college curriculum that leverages a skill set synergy for easier entrance into such a position. Engineering combined with a master's degree in business administration would be one example. Executive managers we know in the healthcare industry went to medical school first. At

Anthony's last firm, the owners were both medical doctors and biomechanical engineers.

This is a good segue to the powerful effect various combinations of expertise can have on a career: the Power Alley Mash-Up!

Skill Set Synergies: The Power Alley Mash-Up

I've taken you through the Power Alleys and the wide variety of career options within each one. I truly believe that there is an appropriate selection within one of the four Power Alleys that would be a good fit for the vast majority of college-bound individuals. Also remember that by the time a college and career path is specifically selected, you and your child will have been discussing, planning, and "grooming" for that targeted area.

With all that said, many won't find the "fit" they are looking for within the Power Alleys. It is for this reason we introduce to you something we call Skill Set Synergies, or the Power Alley Mash-Up. The concept here is to combine one of the Power Alleys with an area of study more in tune with your child's strength and personality. We believe that having a foundation and understanding of at least one Power Alley can super-charge a career in an altogether different field. This practice is the cornerstone of many success stories in executive management.

A good friend is a pharmaceutical salesperson (medical Power Alley). She has done well at this profession for many years. In the last few years she has seen job security erode in the drug sales industry. In fact, wholesale layoffs have been the norm in many cases for what once was a secure and lucrative career choice. In what turned out to be a "stroke of luck" by her own admission, a trip to China years ago set her on a course of study that now makes all the difference in the world. She decided to learn Mandarin, and now is relatively proficient. As a result, her degree and experience in technical sales, plus the unique ability to communicate with the

Chinese, makes her one of the most sought after and highly compensated in her field.

In finance, *Bloomberg* magazine typically profiles a successful industry player each month. In a recent article, *Bloomberg* profiled an investment banker who came from an operations background in the mining industry. Pairing his mining expertise with a MBA in finance, the featured individual joined an investment bank in its mining industry practice.

Even more inventive and successful, one of our case studies, Jeff Bezos, earned degrees in computer science and engineering and worked on Wall Street before founding Amazon.com.

The key to designing an individualized Power Alley: Find a particular area in which your child has interest and can excel, and combine it with a Power Alley.

Foreign languages, for example, are a pretty obvious addition. In fact, we would suggest your child learn a foreign language as a matter of course. This builds in a synergy from the very beginning. Yet there are lots more possibilities, and we encourage you to brainstorm.

We believe the following areas of expertise would be very powerful when combined with any field of study:

- Foreign language skills
- Computer science
- Social media expertise
- Technology
- Finance
- Sales
- Accounting
- Logistics
- Statistics

- Entrepreneurship
- Legal environment
- Engineering

You are now aware of the Power Alleys—the pathways taken by so many who now command 10 percent of the wealth in America. You are also aware of Skill Set Synergies that combine value-added skills to create additional pathways, or enhance the existing ones.

The need that remains is a method for putting this all together. In the following chapter, we will introduce a framework that allows you to see what needs to be done from start to finish.

Doesn't it feel awesome to break the College Unicorn myth and use this knowledge to launch your child on a path to career and financial independence?

Chapter 6
The Program

"All glory comes from daring to begin."–Eugene F. Ware

We've covered a lot of ground on our way to disseminating this powerful information about college majors and their worth. The framework for starting your child on a path to career and financial independence has evolved from analyzing the backgrounds and education of the wealthy to a recipe that can be utilized by all. Reflect upon the evolution of Optimal Career Planning and reinforce your desire to adopt, learn, and execute the program.

No human pursuit has ever been truly life-changing without belief in that pursuit, along with a wholehearted commitment to it. We wrote *The College Unicorn* based on our complete belief in its ability to deliver a satisfying life free of financial worry. You know our belief is rooted in our research and our observation of those already enjoying such freedom and the pride they exude having gotten there.

In many ways our program is no more novel than completing career paths that have been traveled before. Our primary focus has been to expose you to that which you may have observed on your own, but never associated with your own child's destiny. We also seek to get you to overcome your inertia, to take action, to set goals, and to guide your child to a lifetime of learning and high achievement. Praying and hoping for the best for your child is a losing strategy in the current economic disproportion, at least when it comes to career planning and maximizing return on investment of your tuition dollars.

We have reached that moment when all that you have read in *The College Unicorn* comes down to one simple question: "Will you decide to guide your child down a path that has career and financial independence as its result?"

Making the Decision

Belief and commitment toward achieving a goal begins with a choice. There is no disputing who the wealthiest top 10 percent are and how they got there. There is no disputing those in the top 10 percent are career and financially independent and much better off than the remaining 90 percent. There is also no disputing the continued migration of wealth toward the top ten percentile. As a result, it is easy to conclude that the route to a life free of financial worry is one that places an individual within, or as close to, that income group.

Early on we warned that the College Unicorn program was not for everyone. Proceed knowing that any and all of your effort in applying these principles will pay your children lifelong dividends.

So you've been informed and you've been warned: now decide.

Understand the Concept

In order to reach the goals *The College Unicorn* sets before you, you will have to have a solid understanding of our concept. This is a good time for you to review previous portions of our book. As an alternative to such backtracking now, here's a summary of all you really need to know.

An overarching concept of *The College Unicorn* is:

> *A life filled with career and financial worry is unnecessary. Aiming for the top 10 percent in any pursuit encourages extra effort and will be met with extra rewards. Indeed, going through life trying to do the bare minimum or settling for an average job will not lead to material or psychological rewards. Traditional college planning has failed to prepare*

*students for a life free from such worry and, in fact,
may even compound the problem.*

The College Unicorn exposes a "better way." The logical steps toward our goal are these:

- Career and financial independence resides within the top 10 percent of the population.
- The career pathway(s) to the top 10 percent are the Power Alleys.
- The Power Alleys are careers in medicine, finance, the law, and executive management.
- Aspiring to one of the Power Alleys requires The Formula.
- The Formula is: Native Ability + Smart Work + Power Alley + Luck = Top 10 Percent.

Conduct a Self-Assessment

Marketing and contemporary business expert par excellence, Seth Godin, was quoted in an article on Business Insider (www.businessinsider.com) titled "If You're an Average Worker, You're Going Straight to the Bottom." In the interview he says, "If you're going to say 'I'm an average guy doing average work,' we'll find somebody cheaper than you."

What we're saying is now is **not** the time to be average, or do average work. Aim to achieve at the top 10 percent level in your field or endeavor. Keep that thought in the back of your mind as you proceed.

If you and your child have all the tools necessary to execute our plan, and you've given yourself plenty of time, you are lucky! Most of us will discover deficiencies in ourselves, our children, and our timing. It is best to be honest with yourself at the outset; this will expose the areas that need the most work. Very few start with all the tools and preparation they need, but personal improvement is a life-long journey. Our research into those in the top 10 percent revealed shortcomings that had to be corrected or improved.

We will assist you with a more thorough self-assessment process in the future. But for now, there are two variables in The Formula which provide a good place to start. We discussed "native ability," which can have a wide-ranging definition. By "native ability" we do not mean a high IQ, but you and your child's ability to be driven and committed. That is not to say that being smart is not a head start, but we believe success can also be achieved through hard work, dedication, and perseverance.

In 2008, Canadian journalist, bestselling author, and speaker Malcolm Gladwell published the book _Outliers_ in which he presents a plausible and well-supported theory that through ten thousand hours of deliberate practice anyone can perform at the expert level in almost any field. This specific theory is that of psychologist K. Anders Ericsson, PhD, a professor at Florida State University, who published his team's findings in the _Cambridge Handbook of Expertise and Expert Performance_. The truth is that anyone can be an expert in any field if they'll invest the time.

You will also have to be honest about your own work ethic—if you have high hopes for your child as we do, you too will have to possess or develop the habits embodied by the most successful.

In the formula for success we address a variable called "smart work". Hard work and dedication can be taught and developed within all of us. The "smart" part of the term refers to being efficient and making good choices. Again, these attributes can be introduced, practiced, and incorporated in one's behavior. Assessing one's ability to work smart, and improving on that ability, makes executing your plan that much easier.

Many times the self-assessment process will come down to common sense. Hopefully we all have a general understanding of what it takes to be successful. What we don't usually have is the ability to be honest about areas in which we need improvement, and then taking steps to make those improvements.

Do Your Homework

It's just as important to do your own homework as it is to monitor the quality and timeliness of your student's homework. It is impossible to execute the plans *The College Unicorn* has in store without a continuous desire to learn on your part. The ability to succeed will rest in your desire to stay involved and on top of the latest information your child may need. We trust that this will be a satisfying journey for you as well, and what better example for your child to follow than a parent who's constantly learning.

We encourage you to go beyond the research we have done for you. Research for yourself to see that the distribution of wealth has been concentrating for decades. Prove to yourself that of those in the top 10 percent, many have used a Power Alley to get there. If you monitor current events you'll see for yourself that a many of college graduates today are struggling to find a job, are moving back home, and are deep in debt.

We encourage you to study economics or finance, and keep abreast of current trends and changes in the job market. Share and discuss this information with your child; use every opportunity to add to their skills and knowledge.

Establish a Solid Foundation

It has been said that in order to build a structure that stands the test of time, you need a solid foundation. Building a career that provides financial independence is no different—only a solid foundation will provide the basis for all that needs to be accomplished to get there. Continuous self-improvement will always be a "work in progress" for you and your child, but having this awareness when starting out is a great help.

Part of the self-assessment process will focus on you. Since you will be an integral part of your child's plans and ability to succeed, your own "foundation" must be analyzed. Questions you must ask yourself include: How is my relationship, in general, with my child? Am I leading by example, in a way that my child would want to emulate? How much career planning have I done so far? What is my plan for my child; is it similar to the "college and pray" plan we introduced earlier? Am I raising my child in a way that is rooted in career and life preparation? No doubt many of these questions will be essential, but be honest and improve those areas that need it.

There are so many things that can be done to give your child a base from which to succeed. Let's take a look at a couple of examples.

Recently we attended a friend's birthday party. Among the guests were a number of families including young children. When it came time to sing the "Happy Birthday" song, one set of parents asked if it would be okay if their three sons (aged five to nine) gave it a try. The celebrant agreed, and the three boys sang the song...in Mandarin! How about that for a "head start" for these young children?

Another friend's teenage daughter is sixteen and a junior in high school. Our discussions revealed that the parent's plan for this bright teen was nothing more than "college and pray." After a number of discussions with us, this teen and her parents created a focus on a specific career path. She has redirected her high school courses toward a career in finance, including advanced placement courses in statistics, finance, foreign language, and technical writing. Her new focus has gained her an invitation to join an elite group of students poised to become National Merit Scholars, and she is personally leading a campaign to apply for admission and scholarships at top business schools.

The opportunity to set a solid "foundation" is everywhere!

Pick a Power Alley

In order to hit a target, you actually have to have one. Aiming at something that doesn't exist is obviously futile, just as shooting at a target we cannot see is pointless. That's why picking a Power Alley is so crucial. Without a goal in mind, or a planned vision, it is impossible to reach a specific career destination, or any destination for that matter. And yet, it is all too common for students to take off on what is allegedly a career path, with no specific goal in mind.

We've discussed the Power Alleys, so you are now familiar with them. You also know we believe that orienting toward one of the Power Alleys is of crucial importance. Once you have done your research regarding the Power Alleys and completed an assessment with your student, it is time to choose.

Document a Plan

Planning for a career and life free of financial worry is a planning and educational effort no less rigorous or detailed than one necessary for completing a major construction project, like a bridge or a high-rise building.

List every item and action that is necessary to achieve your stated goal, i.e. books to be read, career research to be conducted, mentor possibilities, new languages to learn, schools to be researched, etc., should all go in the plan. Write your plan down and be detailed, including start and end dates for accomplishments. On a set schedule, document your progress. Your written plan will keep you and your child motivated and organized. Deadlines will be established and accountability maintained.

As you document your progress, look at your level of effort and commitment. Be honest with yourselves about how well you are adhering to the plan, and which deficiencies were due to circumstances beyond your control versus those that were due to your own lack of commitment. More importantly, what you do to recognize, adapt, and correct those areas that are lacking will be critical to consistent achievement.

Take Action

Now it is time to take action. Many times the hardest part of a project is just getting started, yet we urge you to do so. Each day the facts and statistics continue to prove that achieving real success with traditional career and college planning is a very flawed strategy.

These ongoing findings will only solidify the concept, pathways, and process contained in *The College Unicorn*. Getting started now can begin to ensure that your child or student creates an opportunity for a life free of financial worry.

In the next chapter we provide specific actions you can take now in order to start the process. Every day there are opportunities to prepare yourself and your child for what it will take to execute what we believe is "a better way" to a better life.

Chapter 7
21 Tips to Keep Your College Grad From Moving Back Home

You've made it to the last chapter, so it's safe to say that you are intent on making the strategic decision to leverage your student's education by choosing an optimal career path. How do you plan on following it all the way, right through graduation day? What happens after graduation?

As a parent of a college-bound child you want to be sure that you're doing everything you can to ensure that they are developing the mindset and behaviors of those who are most successful. Most importantly you want your student to be in the ranks of college grads that do not move back home.

Starting early is certainly the best recipe for success, but it is never too late. Capturing the mind and interest of teenagers can be challenging, but every effort you make to open their eyes relative to the current economic realities, the challenges they face, and tactics to overcome these challenges, is well worth it.

All these concepts and behaviors can be learned, and learning these is vital. Let's take a simple example that we have noticed by observing various generations:

We can all agree that wearing a seatbelt in a car is vital to motoring safety.

- Senior citizens continually need to be reminded to fasten their seatbelts.

- Middle-aged people often fasten their belt once they've begun their trip.
- Teenagers immediately fasten their belt on being seated in any vehicle.

The reason teens are so conscientious about this critical personal safety practice is due to a lifetime of direct parental involvement and societal reinforcement. Obviously, seniors and midlife individuals were not "coached" so well in this area. The fact teens have been provided with this coaching makes us feel good, lessens worry, and most importantly, reduces their risk of injury.

One can project this example over a wide range of other influenced behaviors, including those vital to career and financial independence. Let's start with the following tips.

1. Make Life Fun – This step is important to teach, because life and work should be fun. Top performers typically "love" life and have fun at work and beyond. Early exposure to a wide variety of life experiences, from recreation and travel to hard work and learning, makes these practices enjoyable. You noticed I slipped in "hard work," and kids do not find that fun, do they? Well, maybe not at first, but if you emphasize the "payoff,"—such as vacations, good food, sports, toys, concerts, and so on—and then they receive one, we are beginning a "cycle" that will become invaluable. Always tie these "payoff activities" back to the work they do and financial capability. Have them book the tickets, see the price, and explain where the money comes from. Have them calculate the "tip" and total the bill at a restaurant (basic math skills). Have them fill the gas tank, shop for groceries,

or execute a major purchase. Discuss the cost of living, and explain how you became able to pay for it all, and if you cannot, the mistakes you made. You want to do everything you can to help your child succeed, but you also want them to be acutely aware of what success "costs." One main reason they are going to school, getting a job, and earning money is so they can "enjoy life," right after they get their own place.

2. Set Their Sights High – Someone said, "Dreams are free, you might as well aim high." Just like you've impressed on your children that they will go to college, you need to share that you expect them to reach their full potential and pick a career path that not only allows them to become self-sufficient, but leads to a career that can support their dreams. Talk about life after college, lifestyle expectations, where they plan to live, and what will be needed to get there.

3. Subsidize Savings– They exist, but you do not see many piggy banks anymore. When your friends have children, buy one in pink or blue that says "COLLEGE" on the side. Saving is a lost art in our world today, and the lack thereof is crushing those who never learned how. If you have young children, make frequent stops at the piggy bank when they find a coin or complete a chore. Empty it from time to time and have them count their "savings". Praise the act and provide a reward. A brilliant financial blogger, David Merkel of the www.alephblog.com, provides his children with accounts in the "Bank of Dad" in which he offers 5 percent interest on his children's savings. It's a terrific idea because he's building a great habit early in life and teaching delayed

gratification. If your children are teens or preteens, take them to the bank and open a savings account today! Create online access so they can track their balance and learn about interest. Find ways to make deposits, from portions of gifts, odd jobs around the house, or from selling on eBay. Get creative and get them saving. As a team, begin to establish a budget and financial plan for college and beyond. Avoid looking at college graduation as the finish line. All this sets the stage for domestic independence when college is nothing more than a memory.

4. Expose Your Kids to Real World Finance – Share your financial information with your children as early as possible so they can grasp "paying the bills" like rent, utilities, insurance, taxes, along with the concept of "pocket money." Show them your income and have them pay bills with you online. These will teach lessons in cash flow. Explain what a bill is and why it is necessary. You may even find some savings as you review your expenditures with your child. Take a long time to appreciate the total, and explain all you have to do to generate this amount month after month, year after year. The more they realize that everything costs money and that earning money is a personal responsibility, the better they will be at making it happen for themselves.

5. Encourage Your Kids to Get a Job or Start a Business – The sooner your child gets involved in something that can be defined as a "job"—and this needs to happen way before college—they will be more suited to work during and after college. Jobs—at home for the youngest ones, in food service or retail for teens—all begin the accumulation of vital skills such as job hunting, interviewing, interpersonal

skills, and managing their newly found income. This first job will also influence the things they "like" and "dislike" about work. A favorable result would be hearing, "Dad, I sure don't want to flip burgers or paint houses all my life."

6. Encourage Them to Aim for the Top 10 Percent – Whether we like it or not, the concentration of wealth has been applied to the top 10 percent of the US population for the last forty years. In order to focus on a career that not only provides independence for your children, but allows them to reach their dreams, these top career choices must be explored. Bring the future into the present by discussing where they might live, what industries they might work in, and develop a list of potential options. This important step begins to set the plan for high school planning, college planning, internships, summer jobs, and friendships with other high achievers with similar interests.

7. Teach Networking – The world today is all about relationships and networking. If you have a shy kid, find ways to be more comfortable in social situations. Facebook and Twitter are okay, but "in person" communication is still more important. Have your child interview a few professionals who are currently working in top positions that he or she is most interested in. Everyone knows a successful business owner or some other successful professional. Get your child to chat with them soon. Most successful people have real-world experiences, lessons, and rules of thumb that they've used to achieve their successes.

8. Encourage Fitness – Healthy people perform better, are typically more attractive, and are more likely to possess high

self-esteem and exude self-confidence. Formal athletics are great for teaching healthy competition, leadership, hard work, dedication, the ability to bounce back after a loss, and reward for the effort. If formal athletics are not "in the cards," not to worry, one can make use of that time to work on some of these tips! So becoming a "health nut" or "gym rat" is not necessary, but make sure activity is included in your child's routine. It has been said you should "break a sweat" at least once a day. This could be raking the yard or riding a bicycle. Do it with your kid—it can be a bonding experience.

During College:

9. Convert Their Room – The day they move out, figure out what their bedroom will now become. Maybe it's a workout room, a study, an office, or a guest bedroom. This sends a very clear message of your intentions. It is also psychological reinforcement that moving back home will not be a Plan B.

10. Start the Job Countdown – This is a continuation of the expectation you set with your child before they started college: Do not give up. It's the same tactics/rewards/support system that you used so they were able to complete high school with good grades and a record of achievement. College is only a stepping stone to the goal of finding gainful employment. While in college, practicing hard work, learning to add value, problem solving, and networking is the goal.

11. Build a Resume – Most college grads start thinking about their resume the last semester of school because finding a job is the next step. Why not start drafting your resume your freshman year? Senior year in high school? Build solid experiences employers will find unique and be as innovative as possible during this time. Have it ready and keep their resume in mind for additional updates.

12. Write Cover Letters – Imagine if you were an employer and prospective employees started writing you cover letters with their resume years in advance of graduation? Every year...telling you what they've learned, how they will add value when you hire them, and how much they are looking forward to working with you. With the current job market, this is a smart tactic for everyone.

13. Continue to Network – Ever hear the phrase "It´s not what you know, it's who you know?" You will need to explain to your college student that the friends they are making in college could be their colleagues tomorrow. They want to connect with people that will help them in their chosen field down the road. Having the bond and connection of being friends in college goes a long way toward getting to the top of that applicant list. Additionally, teach them to help others achieve their goals, encourage their friends' high achievements, and learn to appreciate others' accomplishments without envy. A network of highly successful friends can provide valuable advice, aid, support, and introductions for the rest of their life.

14. Learn How to Interview – In a week's time you can learn all the best practices on how to answer questions, shake hands,

and do the interview dance. There is a plethora of advice on bookshelves or on the Internet teaching interviewing skills. If your student starts rehearsing these skills early they will outshine the competition. Get out the video camera and practice, practice, practice.

15. Dress for Success – Teach the importance of having your interview apparel ready to go months before your first interview. Maybe you could buy them new shoes, just for interviewing, an admirable watch, and support the practice of being impeccably groomed at a moment's notice. If their position requires that they have certain tools, make sure they get them before they need them. If they look and sound like they already have the job, your student will be miles above the competition.

After College:

16. Stay Organized – It's easy to lose track when the formal schedules of college disappear. Keep a calendar, set goals, and maintain focus. Build a job-hunting database listing where you want to work, who has openings, and with whom you've made contact.

17. Teach Them How to Live Cheap – Everyone starts out broke or even in debt after school. Credit card companies will be prospecting your grad while in school or shortly thereafter. The mantra should be: Spend less, save more. Until they are employed, your student will need to understand that living frugally by choice is better than by force.

18. Get Their Foot in the Door – The point is that every adult needs an income; otherwise, they become a dependent. Many super-successful people have failed at initial forays into the work or business world, but they have learned valuable lessons along the way. In some careers, senior people call entry-level jobs requiring hard work and little pay "paying your dues." We believe that establishing in your student a philosophy of hard work, a work ethic of delivering superior value, and an understanding that no one owes them a living will be an important mindset for high achievement. The job market is challenging, but any position where one can learn the business, make contacts, and delight his or her employer can parlay this early opportunity into future success.

So they've already moved home (or are about to)...

19. Initiate a Loving, but Serious Discussion – They want to move back in... what happened? You need to find out what went wrong. Saying "I just can't find a job" is not the answer. Do they want to go to grad school, do they need a little break, or are they just plain lazy? You need to have a serious discussion with your grad at this point. You are no longer obligated to provide them with anything because they are now an adult.

20. Set Clear Expectations – If they must move back home, make them pay whatever rent they can afford. Make them buy what food they eat. They must do their fair share of chores, and they must look for work. You need to explain that there is a trade-off for allowing them access to your house. Have them set goals regarding their future plans of

moving out with a time line. Keep track of milestones relative to their progress.

21. Maintain Accountability – If your kids are wearing or driving their paychecks or are acting any way in contrast with their stated goals, you need to call them on it. You hold the key at this point just as you have in the past. If your college grad is living at home, rest assured, they will take whatever you give them.

Many actions and principles have been offered here and they will put you and your child well on the way to financial and career independence. Some of these principles may seem overreaching or they are points you are already aware of. If some of these suggestions seem as though we are overreacting, let us remind you of the current economic times and job market, where one cannot prepare enough for acquiring that first position after college. All these tips are not only possible, but necessary, and are common attributes of individuals who have achieved long-lasting career success. If these "21 Tips" seem like something you already knew, then let them be a call to action. Imagine the pride you will feel when you help put your child on the path to realize his or her dreams.

Additional information can be found at:

CollegeUnicorn.com

OptimalCareer.com

IKnowYoullRemember.com

Bibliography

"Afraid of College? The Two Biggest Reasons Why Americans Don't Get a Four-Year Degree." Afraid of College? The Two Biggest Reasons Why Americans Don't Get a Four-Year Degree. N.p., n.d. Web. 04 July 2012. http://myfamilyfinances.net/2012/06/afraid-of-college-the-two-biggest-reasons-why-americans-dont-get-a-four-year-degree.

"Alan Dershowitz." Wikipedia. Wikimedia Foundation, 07 Mar. 2012. Web. 08 July 2012. <http://en.wikipedia.org/wiki/Alan_Dershowitz>.

"Chelsea Clinton." Wikipedia. Wikimedia Foundation, 07 May 2012. Web. 08 July 2012. <http://en.wikipedia.org/wiki/Chelsea_Clinton>.

"David Tepper." Wikipedia. Wikimedia Foundation, 07 Mar. 2012. Web. 08 July 2012. <http://en.wikipedia.org/wiki/David_Tepper>.

Ellsberg, Michael. The Education of Millionaires: It's Not What You Think and It's Not Too Late. New York: Portfolio/Penguin, 2011. Print.

Ericsson, K. Anders. The Cambridge Handbook of Expertise and Expert Performance. Cambridge: Cambridge UP, 2006. Print.

"Executive Employment Agreements - Negotiating and Structuring Executive Employment Agreements." Executive Employment Agreements - Negotiating and Structuring Executive Employment Agreements. N.p., n.d. Web. 08 July 2012. <http://www.executiveemploymentagreements.com/>.

"F. Lee Bailey." Wikipedia. Wikimedia Foundation, 27 June 2012. Web. 08 July 2012. <http://en.wikipedia.org/wiki/F._Lee_Bailey>.

Giang, Vivian. "SETH GODIN: If You're An Average Worker, You're Going Straight To The Bottom." Business Insider. N.p., 9 Jan. 2012. Web. 08 July 2012. <http://www.businessinsider.com/if-youre-an-average-worker-in-this-forever-recession-youre-going-straight-to-the-bottom-2012-1>.

Gladwell, Malcolm. Outliers: The Story of Success. New York: Little, Brown and, 2008. Print.

Goudreau, Jenna. "How I Became A 21-Year-Old Business Executive." Forbes. Forbes Magazine, 09 May 2012. Web. 04 July 2012. <http://www.forbes.com/sites/jennagoudreau/2012/05/09/how-i-became-a-21-year-old-business-executive/>.

"Henry Kravis." Wikipedia. Wikimedia Foundation, 07 Mar. 2012. Web. 08 July 2012. <http://en.wikipedia.org/wiki/Henry_Kravis>.

"Henry Paulson." Wikipedia. Wikimedia Foundation, 07 Aug. 2012. Web. 08 July 2012. <http://en.wikipedia.org/wiki/Henry_Paulson>.

"The Higher Education Bubble [Kindle Edition]." Amazon.com: The Higher Education Bubble EBook: Glenn Harlan Reynolds: Kindle Store. N.p., n.d. Web. 04 July 2012. <http://www.amazon.com/The-Higher-Education-Bubble-ebook/dp/B0088Q9TAU/ref=kinw_dp_keie=UTF8>.

"Hillary Rodham Clinton." Wikipedia. Wikimedia Foundation, 07 July 2012. Web. 08 July 2012. <http://en.wikipedia.org/wiki/Hillary_Rodham_Clinton>.
"How the Rich Became the über Rich." CNNMoney. Cable News Network, 22 Feb. 2011. Web. 08 July 2012. <http://money.cnn.com/2011/02/22/news/economy/income_inequality/index.htm>.

"Humble Student of the Markets." : Portrait of the Artist as a Young Slave. N.p., n.d. Web. 04 July 2012. <http://humblestudentofthemarkets.blogspot.com/2012/06/portrait-of-artist-as-young-slave.html>.

"James Simons." Wikipedia. Wikimedia Foundation, 07 Aug. 2012. Web. 08 July 2012. <http://en.wikipedia.org/wiki/James_Simons>.

"J. Craig Venter." Wikipedia. Wikimedia Foundation, 07 June 2012. Web. 08 July 2012. <http://en.wikipedia.org/wiki/J._Craig_Venter>.

"Jeff Bezos." Wikipedia. Wikimedia Foundation, 07 Aug. 2012. Web. 08 July 2012. <http://en.wikipedia.org/wiki/Jeff_Bezos>.

"Johnnie Cochran." Wikipedia. Wikimedia Foundation, 07 Mar. 2012. Web. 08 July 2012. <http://en.wikipedia.org/wiki/Johnnie_Cochran>.

Kalwarski, Tara. "NUMBERS THE BENEFITS—AND COSTS— OF COLLEGE."Business Week. Bloomberg, n.d. Web. 8 July 2012. <http://images.businessweek.com/mz/10/12/20100322_numbers.pdf?chan=magazine+channel_the+week+in+business>.

"Kennedy Family." Wikipedia. Wikimedia Foundation, 07 May 2012. Web. 08 July 2012. <http://en.wikipedia.org/wiki/Kennedy_family>.

Marcelino, Francisco. "Redecard Profit Beats Estimates After Headcount Reduction."Bloomberg. Bloomberg.com, 18 Apr. 2012. Web. 08 July 2012. <http://www.bloomberg.com/news/2012-04-18/redecard-profit-beats-estimates-after-headcount-reduction-1-.html>.

Merkel, David. "The Aleph Blog." The Aleph Blog. N.p., n.d. Web. 08 July 2012. <http://alephblog.com/>.

Recession, NEW YORK (CNNMoney) -- Despite the Great. "Number of Millionaires Is Projected to Rise

Rapidly." CNNMoney. Cable News Network, 05 May 2011. Web. 08 July 2012. <http://money.cnn.com/2011/05/05/pf/millionaire_rise/index.htm>.

"Required Salary Calculator." The Salary Calculator. N.p., n.d. Web. 08 July 2012. <http://us.thesalarycalculator.co.uk/lifestyle.php>.

"Robert Shapiro (lawyer)." Wikipedia. Wikimedia Foundation, 07 Mar. 2012. Web. 08 July 2012. <http://en.wikipedia.org/wiki/Robert_Shapiro_(lawyer)>.

Roberts, William. "What Can We Learn From The Real Life Doogie Howser?" I Know You'll Remember. N.p., 5 June 2012. Web. 08 July 2012. <http://iknowyoullremember.com/what-can-we-learn-from-the-real-life-doogie-howser/>.

Roberts, Williams. "Working Smart | 6 Places for Students to Learn Better." I Know You'll Remember. N.p., n.d. Web. 04 July 2012. <http://iknowyoullremember.com/working-smart-6-places-for-students-to-learn-better>.

"Rockefeller Family." Wikipedia. Wikimedia Foundation, 07 Aug. 2012. Web. 08 July 2012. <http://en.wikipedia.org/wiki/Rockefeller_family>.

"Rothschild Family." Wikipedia. Wikimedia Foundation, 07 Aug. 2012. Web. 08 July 2012. <http://en.wikipedia.org/wiki/Rothschild_family>.

"Table 33. Actual and Projected Numbers for Bachelor's Degrees Conferred by Postsecondary Degree-granting Institutions, by Sex of Recipient: 1995-96 through 2020-21." Table 33. Actual and Projected Numbers for Bachelor's Degrees Conferred by Postsecondary Degree-granting Institutions, by Sex of Recipient: 1995-96 through 2020-21. N.p., n.d. Web. 04 July 2012. http://nces.ed.gov/programs/projections/projections2020/tables/table_33.asp?referrer=list.

"Timothy Geithner." Wikipedia. Wikimedia Foundation, 07 July 2012. Web. 08 July 2012. <http://en.wikipedia.org/wiki/Timothy_Geithner>.

"UnCollege." UnCollege. N.p., n.d. Web. 08 July 2012. <http://www.uncollege.org/>.

U.S. Office of Tax Analysis. Department of Treasury. Jobs and Income Growth of Top Earners and the Causes of Changing Income Inequality: Evidence from U.S. Tax Return Data. By Jon Bakija and Bradley T. Heim. N.p.: n.d., 2009. Print.

"Warren Buffet." Wikipedia. Wikimedia Foundation, 24 June 2012. Web. 08 July 2012. <http://en.wikipedia.org/wiki/Warren_Buffet>.

Wolff,

"Who Rules America." Wikipedia. Wikimedia Foundation, 25 May 2012. Web. 04 July 2012. http://en.wikipedia.org/wiki/Who_Rules_America.

"William Jefferson Clinton." Wikipedia. Wikimedia Foundation, 07 Apr. 2012. Web. 08 July 2012. <http://en.wikipedia.org/wiki/William_Jefferson_Clinton>.

"With You in Mind, Issue #16 - August, 2009 -- Rich People: What Do They Have in Common?" With You in Mind, Issue #16 - August, 2009 -- Rich People: What Do They Have in Common? N.p., n.d. Web. 08 July 2012. http://www.way-of-the-mind.com/With_You_in_Mind-mind-newsletter-august09.html.

Wolff, Edward N. Recent Trends in Household Wealth in the United States: Rising Debt and the Middle-Class-Squeeze - an Update to 2007. Working paper no. 589. Annandale-on-Hudson: Levy Economics Institutes, 2010. Print.

Wolverson, Raya. "Why Can'☐™t College Grads Find Better Jobs?" Business. Time, Inc., 20 May 2010. Web. 08 July 2012. <http://business.time.com/2011/05/20/why-cant-college-grads-find-better-jobs/>.

34505346R00054

Made in the USA
Lexington, KY
08 August 2014